From Fear to Love

Breaking Free From Control

By Jaziz Gutierrez

Copyright Page

From Fear to Love: Breaking Free from Control
Copyright © 2025 by **Jaziz Gutierrez**
All rights reserved.

No portion of this book may be reproduced, stored in a retrieval system, or transmitted in any form or by any means—electronic, mechanical, photocopy, recording, or otherwise—without prior written permission from the publisher, except for brief quotations used in reviews or articles.

Scripture quotations marked *KJV* are taken from the **Holy Bible, King James Version**, public domain.
Scripture quotations marked *NKJV* are taken from the **New King James Version®**, Copyright © 1982 by Thomas Nelson. Used by permission. All rights reserved.

ISBN 979-8-9863357-6-6

Published by **Warrior Princess Publishing**
Printed in the United States of America

Cover design by Jaziz Gutierrez
Interior design by Warrior Princess Publishing

For more information, visit:
www.jazizgutierrez.com

Table of Contents

Dedication i
Author's Introduction ii
About the Author iv
Before We Begin: How We Try to Stay in Control 1
Heart Check: What's Driving My Reactions? 4
How Fear Feeds the Cycle of Pain 12
Understanding the Four Control Styles 14
How to Use This Devotional 15
A Letter from the Father 18
A Prayer of Release From Fear 19
Day 1 The Battle Between Fear and Faith 20
Day 2 Power That Protects, ...24
Day 3 Breaking the Habit of Criticism 28
Day 4 Fear's Quiet Twin 32
Day 5 When Pain Becomes Power 36
Day 6 Energy Draining People 40
Day 7 Name That Drama 44
Day 8 Repentance as Freedom 48
Day 9 Walking in the Light 52
Day 10 Restored Connection 56
Day 11 From Control to Godfidence 60
Day 12 Staying Connected 64
Day 13 Filling the Empty Places 68

Day 14 Letting Go of the False Self 72
Day 15 Trading lies for God's Truth 76
Day 16 Forgiving Our Debtors 81
Day 17 The Armor of Peace 86
Day 18 Learning to Stay Soft 90
Day 19 Speaking Truth Without Control 94
Day 20 The Right Kind of Thirst 98
Day 21 Letting Go of the Door 102
Day 22 Love Without Strings Attached 106
Day 23 Trusting God with Your Growth 110
Day 24 The Rest of Faith 114
Day 25 Becoming the River 118
Day 26 Gratitude In The Midst of Pain 122
Day 27 Joy Through Pain 126
Day 28 Stewarding the Oil in Our Life 130
Day 29 Beauty for Ashes 134
Day 30 All Things Work Together 138

Dedication

To my friend Paul Saumure (Paul the Grateful),
who taught me that we don't have to struggle for love, attention, or someone's energy, because it is more blessed to give than to receive.

He was the first to introduce these concepts to me and showed me a humble way to end my day:

"Lord, what did people have to lose in order that I might win?"

In this self-evaluation, not only do we address our self-centeredness daily, but we also humbly repent for our shortcomings and our control dramas, in order that we may learn to walk in a more excellent way. Thank you, Paul, for not only showing me this way, but also role-modeling it for me.

I also want to dedicate this to all the wounded ones—
those who have longed for love but didn't know how to receive it, who searched for connection yet felt safer alone. To those whose fear became control, and whose control pushed away the very love they desired.

To those whose fear became control,
and whose control pushed away the very love they desired.

This book is for you.

Join our ranks and our journey of healing—
learning to trust, to release, and to understand.

May you discover that you were never unlovable,
only unhealed…
and that perfect love was pursuing you all along.

Author's Introduction

"We love because He first loved us."
— 1 John 4:19

This book was born from my own struggle to understand love in the midst of control, fear, and codependency. For much of my life, I didn't realize how deeply fear had shaped my relationships—how often I gave too much, stayed too long, or tried to fix what wasn't mine to fix. I didn't see that control and codependency are two sides of the same coin: both rooted in fear, both desperate for love.

Like many empaths and givers, I tend to attract people who take more than they give. I used to think that was my purpose—to help, to heal, to carry everyone's burdens. But over time, I realized that love without boundaries isn't love at all—it's depletion.
When you constantly pour out without receiving, you start running on empty. And when you're empty, you begin attracting people who feed on that emptiness. That's how the cycle continues—fear-driven, anxious, and toxic.

The more I prayed, the more God began to reveal something simple yet profound: We are all trying to fill a space that was meant for our Father's love. Every human heart is searching for that sense of safety and belonging. When we don't know the Father's love, we try to get it from people—and that's when control begins. We start managing relationships like emotional economies, trading energy, approval, and affection just to feel okay.

But this isn't how we were designed to live. God created us to be **rooted and grounded in love**—not fear. Love doesn't control, manipulate, or withdraw. Love gives, receives, and heals.
When we're filled with His love, we stop trying to steal it from others. We stop trying to fix people or manage outcomes.
We learn to let go, to trust, and to love without losing ourselves.

Reading *The Celestine Prophecy* years ago helped me recognize some of these patterns—the control dramas that shape how people interact when they're disconnected from divine love. But what I've learned since then is that the real solution isn't found in human energy—it's found in *God's love*. Only His Spirit can teach us how to stay full without feeding off of others.

This devotional is my heart's offering to anyone who's tired of the cycle—the givers who feel drained, the controllers who feel anxious, and the people who just want peace again. Through these daily readings, you'll learn to identify the ways fear hides behind control, how love heals what fear created, and how to live filled instead of empty.

Because when we finally know Love—*real Love*—we finally know God.

"He who does not love does not know God, for God is love."
1 John 4:8

About the Author

Jaziz Gutierrez is a devoted disciple of Jesus Christ whose journey from codependency and emotional control to freedom in God's love has become the heartbeat of her ministry. Through seasons of prayer, fasting, and quiet obedience, she developed a deep sensitivity to the Holy Spirit that now guides her writing, her teaching, and her life.

Having lived on both sides of the emotional equation—as a giver who attracted takers, and as a partner within controlling relationships—Jaziz has seen firsthand how fear-driven patterns destroy love and drain peace. It was in her own breaking that she found the revelation that now defines her calling: when we don't know our Father's love, we try to extract it from others.

Her heart burns to help people recognize that truth and come home to the One who satisfies. She writes to those who feel unseen, unheard, or unworthy—to those who are tired of managing relationships instead of living in freedom.

Her message is simple and powerful:
We were never created to control others out of fear—
we were created to **become** love out of faith.

By blending Scripture, self-awareness, and Spirit-led healing, Jaziz invites readers into a 30-day journey from fear to freedom, from exhaustion to peace, and from control to connection.

Through every page, you will hear the whisper of a Father who never stopped loving you—
and find courage to live from His fullness, not your emptiness.

Other works by Jaziz Gutierrez include:
The Prince and the Beggar Girl,
Beatitudes of Revival, and her contributions to the Holy Ghost Fire Translation Bible.

Before We Begin:
How We Try to Stay in Control

"**Search me, O God, and know my heart;
test me and know my anxious thoughts.
See if there is any way in me that hurts me,
and lead me in the way everlasting.**"
— Psalm 139:23–24 (paraphrased)

"**He heals the brokenhearted and binds up their wounds.**"
— *Psalm 147 : 3*

"**Whoever loses his life for My sake will find it.**"
— *Matthew 16 : 25*

A Gentle Beginning

Before you take the self-evaluation or dive into the devotionals that follow, pause for a moment and breathe.
This isn't about judging yourself — it's about *getting honest so you can get healed.*

Every control pattern, every fear reaction, every unhealthy coping habit begins in the same place: **pain that was never comforted.**
When pain goes unhealed, it doesn't stay quiet — it becomes the center of our thoughts, our choices, even our relationships.
We start reacting instead of responding, grasping instead of trusting, protecting instead of connecting.

Some people become *controllers* because they're terrified of ever being powerless again. Others become *avoiders* because closeness feels unsafe. And some become *victims* — locked in cycles of pity or despair — because pain has quietly become their identity.

When pain sits at the center of the heart, it begins to demand attention. We try to manage others so we won't feel abandoned, or use guilt to keep love close. That's where **narcissistic behavior** is born — not as arrogance, but as *unhealed pain that turned inward.* It's what happens when the soul says, *"If I stay the focus, I can stay safe."* But that kind of safety becomes a prison.

We all long to feel safe, seen, and understood.
But when those needs aren't met—especially early in life—we learn to *manage love* instead of receiving it. We start using subtle strategies to gain energy, attention, or security from others.
That's what this book calls **control dramas**: predictable patterns that form when fear replaces trust.

Most of us don't realize we're doing it. We just notice tension, exhaustion, or emptiness in our relationships. This devotional will help you uncover the ways control shows up in your heart so that love—real, unconditional love—can flow again.

Jesus came to heal that kind of brokenness. He never shames the hurting; He restores them. He invites us to move from **pain-centered living** to **love-centered freedom.**

A Word of Truth and Hope

You are *not* the sum of what happened to you.
You are not your defenses, your control patterns, or your fears.
You are the beloved child of a Father who knows every scar and still calls you *whole.*

Healing begins when we stop orbiting around our hurt and start revolving around His heart.
Let this devotional become a journey back to that center — where love leads, not pain.

Reflection Before the Test

As you answer the evaluation questions, ask:

- "What pain has shaped how I relate to others?"
- "Where have I made my pain the reason I control, withdraw, or manipulate?"
- "What would it look like to let Jesus be the center instead?"

Don't be afraid of what the Holy Spirit shows you — conviction is never condemnation; it's the sound of the Healer knocking gently on the door of your heart.

Prayer

Father, thank You for seeing every place where pain has tried to sit on the throne of my life.
Today I invite You to become the center again.
Heal what I've used to protect myself.
Teach me to trust Your love instead of my fear.
As I begin this journey, help me see truth without shame and hope without denial.
Amen.

Declaration

I am not my pain.
I am not what happened to me.
I am who God says I am — whole, loved, and free.
Jesus, be the center of my healing and the Lord of my story.

Heart Check: What's Driving My Reactions?

Before we can heal, we must first *see*.
The Holy Spirit reveals what fear hides, not to shame us, but to set us free.

Every control pattern began as survival. It was how we learned to protect ourselves when love felt uncertain. But what once helped us cope may now be blocking the connection and peace we long for.

Take this as a **gentle mirror**, not a judgment.
Pray before you begin:

"Holy Spirit, search me and know me. Show me truth so I can walk in freedom."

How to Use This Self-Evaluation

Rate each statement **1–5** based on how often it feels true for you.
(1 = Never, 5 = Almost Always)

#	Statement	Rating (1–5)
1	I feel anxious when things are out of my control.	☐
2	I get frustrated when people don't do what I expect.	☐
3	I often feel overlooked, misunderstood, or powerless.	☐
4	I use silence or distance when I feel hurt or rejected.	☐
5	I ask a lot of probing or challenging questions when I don't trust someone's motives.	☐

#	Statement	Rating (1–5)
6	I raise my voice, dominate, or push harder when I feel unheard.	☐
7	I replay conversations in my head, imagining what I should have said.	☐
8	I tend to withdraw until others come looking for me.	☐
9	I sometimes use guilt or emotion to make people understand how much they hurt me.	☐
10	I get stuck in overanalyzing instead of expressing what I really feel.	☐
11	I secretly want others to admit they were wrong before I can feel at peace.	☐
12	I feel unsafe when I'm not in control of the outcome.	☐
13	I struggle to apologize without explaining or defending myself.	☐
14	When someone confronts me, I turn it back on them or point out their faults.	☐
15	I sometimes use Scripture or "spiritual talk" to justify my behavior.	☐
16	I find it hard to admit when I've hurt someone, even unintentionally.	☐
17	I tend to make excuses instead of taking ownership when things go wrong.	☐

#	Statement	Rating (1–5)
18	I get defensive when others set boundaries with me.	☐
19	I struggle to empathize when someone else is upset or crying.	☐
20	I need people to agree with me to feel at peace.	☐

Interpreting Your Results

1. Circle or note your **five highest scores.**
2. Identify which **control style(s)** those statements most reflect.
3. Ask the Holy Spirit, *"What am I afraid of losing when I act this way?"*

Your answers aren't meant to label you — they're meant to *locate you.*
Awareness is the first step toward healing.

⚡ The Intimidator

Control style: Force, tone, or dominance

The Intimidator is the most visible of the control styles.
This person tries to feel safe by staying powerful—often through intensity, anger, or aggression. When fear or insecurity rise, control feels like the only option to deal with the fear of losing control. Intimidation is an attempt to get people to back down so you can feel safe and secure, but it comes at a cost: others shrink back, and connection breaks.

This pattern can show up as raised voices, sharp tones, or dominating conversations. It can also appear in quieter forms—like the glare that ends a discussion, the heavy sigh that shuts someone down, or the emotional pressure that says, *"Do it my way or pay the punishment."*
It's the belief that if you stay in charge, you can't be hurt again.

Behind every controlling demand is often a frightened heart saying, *"I don't feel safe."*
That's why this pattern is not about evil intent—it's about self-protection gone too far.
God understands that fear, but He also calls you higher.
He wants to teach you that **true authority flows from peace, not dominance or control.**

Real strength doesn't need to overpower others; it rests in calm confidence.
Jesus showed this kind of strength when He stood before His accusers—silent, composed, and anchored in the Father's love. His authority came from identity, not intimidation.

When the Holy Spirit redeems this pattern, the same passion that once sought to control becomes the courage that protects and empowers others.
You were never meant to rule over people, but to lead through love.

Redeemed Gift: Leadership and courage — healed by humility and peace.
Focus on Devotionals: Days 1, 5, 11, 15, and 23.
Action Step: Notice when intensity rises in your tone, body, or thoughts. Pause before reacting. Breathe, pray, and invite God's peace to fill the space where fear once demanded control.
True power doesn't shout—it trusts God to step in.

🔍 The Interrogator

Control style: Questioning, analyzing, or criticism

You feel safer when you understand everything. If you can figure it out, you can't be hurt. But endless analysis creates distance — not intimacy. When fear disguises itself as "discernment," suspicion and accusation takes over.

God invites you to replace interrogation with intercession — to pray instead of pry. He wants to show you that understanding people isn't as important as *loving* them and trusting God.

Redeemed Gift: Insight and discernment — healed by trust and humility.
Focus on Devotionals: Days 3, 7, 12, 15, and 22.
Action Step: Ask curious, compassionate questions instead of critical ones that are meant to pry into people's lives to make you feel safe.

💔 The Victim

Control style: Helplessness, guilt, or emotional crisis

You've learned that pain brings attention and comfort — but deep down, you just want to feel seen and valued without needing to suffer for love. When fear convinces you that no one cares unless you're broken, sick, or helpless, it keeps you in bondage.

Sometimes this pattern turns into *martyrdom* — quietly making others feel guilty for not rescuing you, or using suffering to stay in control of the connection. But that's not how God designed love to work. Love doesn't require others to suffer with you to prove they care.

God is calling you out of the story of "I can't" and into the truth of "I can through Christ."

You are not a burden to be managed — you're a miracle in process.

Redeemed Gift: Empathy and compassion — healed by courage and faith.

Focus on Devotionals: Days 2, 5, 10, 14, and 28.

Action Step: Speak gratitude aloud for what's going right — not just what's wrong with your life. Believe that what Jesus did for you is enough and declare that you are a warrior in the making.

The Stonewaller

Control style: Silence, withdrawal, or emotional shutdown

You've learned that emotions can be dangerous, so when things get hard, you disappear to feel safe. In the past, silence may have become a way to *punish* those who hurt you or to gain back control when you felt powerless. But over time, that silence can turn into isolation — cutting off not just the person, but your own ability to give and receive love.

Now, you're learning that stepping back doesn't have to mean shutting down. You can choose quiet *without disconnecting*, and space *without severing*.

You're discovering the strength to protect your peace without hardening your heart.

God is teaching you that healthy boundaries are not walls — they're fences with gates. Boundaries keep you safe, but love keeps you open.

He's inviting you to stay present with Him even when emotions rise, and to trust that His presence is your refuge, not avoidance.

Redeemed Gift: Stability, patience, and wisdom — healed by openness.

Focus on Devotionals: Days 4, 9, 13, 16, and 20.

Action Step: Stay in the conversation a few minutes longer before retreating. When you feel triggered, take a deep breath, silently invite the Holy Spirit into that moment, and respond only from peace. Keep boundaries that protect your well-being, but don't build walls that block healing.

Reflection & Scoring Guide

Once you've tallied your responses, reflect on what you see emerging.

Use these prompts to deepen your awareness:

1. What emotions rise up when you feel out of control?
2. How do you react when someone challenges you?
3. Do you apologize quickly or wait for others to come first?
4. Have you ever used anger, guilt, or silence to get your way?
5. Do you feel loved when you're not in charge?
6. When was the last time you listened without defending yourself?
7. Have you ever twisted truth or Scripture to stay "right"?
8. Do you secretly believe people owe you for what you've done for them?
9. How do you respond when someone says "no" to you?
10. What would love — not fear — look like in your next hard moment?

"Healing doesn't come by willpower — it comes by truth. And the truth will set you free." — *John 8:32*

How Fear Feeds the Cycle of Pain

Control dramas rarely exist in isolation. In relationships, one person's fear often awakens the other's. What begins as self-protection can quickly become warfare, two wounded hearts fighting to feel safe and loved. The result is not intimacy but exhaustion, frustration, and isolation.

It's usually easy to see our partner's drama and almost impossible to see our own. We might say, "He's always angry," or "She never talks," without realizing how our reactions keep the pattern alive. Fear meets fear. What was supposed to be love now becomes a battle.

One pushes; the other pulls away. Both are hurting, both are trying to be loved, and both end up lonelier than before.

Example 1 – The Power Struggle:
When an Intimidator raises his voice, the Victim shuts down and cries. The louder he becomes, the smaller she feels—and the smaller she feels, the louder he becomes. Each believes the other is the problem, when in truth, both are protecting their own pain.

Example 2 – The Endless Trial:
An Interrogator demands explanations, thinking that understanding will bring peace. The Stonewaller grows quieter, feeling cornered and unsafe. The silence drives the Interrogator mad; the questioning drives the Stonewaller deeper into hiding.

Example 3 – The Disappearing Act:
Chuck and Marilyn both discovered that silence was their armor. When arguments arose, one of them would leave the room—or the house—hoping the other would chase after them. It was an attempt to control connection through absence. Once they recognized it, they began staying present and owning their feelings. Their honesty became the bridge back to love.

When we recognize that *our partner's control drama triggers ours*, we can begin to break the cycle. Healing starts when even one person chooses to respond differently—to stay, to listen, to soften instead of react.

The opposite of control is not passivity; it's **trust**—trusting that God can protect what we surrender and heal what we release.

Reflection

1. Whose control pattern most triggers yours, and why?
2. What do you usually do when you feel cornered or criticized?
3. Where might you be using withdrawal, silence, or guilt to keep control?
4. What would it look like to let love—not fear—lead the next hard moment?

Prayer

Father, open my eyes to the ways fear still drives my reactions.
When I feel attacked, remind me that I am safe in Your love.
Teach me to stay present when I want to run, gentle when I want to fight, and humble when I want to be right.
Heal the patterns between me and the people I love.
Let Your peace become our new language.
In Jesus' name, amen.

Understanding the Four Control Styles

Now that we can see how fear feeds the cycle of pain, let's look more closely at the patterns that keep it spinning. Each control style began as a way to survive when love felt uncertain — a child's instinct to feel safe, seen, or valued. But when those patterns grow up with us, they become habits that block connection and intimacy.

These are not labels meant to shame you; they're mirrors meant to reveal you. When we understand what fear has been teaching us to do, we can finally invite God to teach us a better way — the way of love, humility, and peace.

You may recognize yourself in one of these four patterns:

- **The Intimidator**, who controls through power and dominance.
- **The Interrogator**, who controls through questions and criticism.
- **The Victim**, who controls through helplessness and guilt.
- **The Stonewaller**, who controls through silence and withdrawal.

Each of these styles has a redemptive side — a divine reflection buried beneath the fear. As you read, don't rush to fix yourself or diagnose others. Instead, ask the Holy Spirit to uncover the truth beneath the behavior and **heal the wound beneath the fear**.

"Perfect love casts out fear." — 1 John 4:18

How to Use This Devotional

"You will seek Me and find Me when you seek Me with all your heart."
— Jeremiah 29:13

This devotional isn't meant to be rushed or read like a checklist. It's a daily conversation between your heart and the heart of God. Each day will meet you where you are and gently lead you deeper—away from fear, control, and striving, and into love, peace, and trust.

Here's how to get the most out of this journey:

---

1. Go Slow and Be Honest

Take your time.
These pages are not for performance—they're for transformation.
If a certain day stirs up emotion, stay there until you feel peace again.
Healing is not about speed; it's about *truth meeting love*.

---

2. Make Space for God

Set aside a few quiet minutes each day—morning, lunch, or before bed.
Turn off distractions, breathe deeply, and invite the Holy Spirit to speak.
Say something simple like, *"Lord, I'm here. Help me see what You see."*

---

3. Read, Reflect, Respond

Each day includes:

- **Scripture Reading** — The foundation for that day's truth.
- **Teaching** — A reflection to guide your heart toward understanding.
- **Reflection Questions** — A space for honesty and self-awareness.
- **Prayer & Deliverance Declaration** — Words to help you align your heart and mind with truth.
- **Action Step** — A small, practical way to walk out what you've learned.

Have a journal or notebook nearby to capture what the Holy Spirit shows you.
This is where much of your healing will take root.

---

4. Don't Just Read—Receive

Some of these topics may touch old wounds or stir hidden pain.
Don't be afraid of that—it's just proof that God is healing you.
When tears come, let them.
When conviction comes, lean in.
This is how transformation happens: love revealing truth and replacing fear.

---

5. Pray Before and After Each Reading

Ask God to open your heart at the start,
and thank Him at the end for what He's uncovering.
You'll begin to notice subtle changes—less tension, more peace,
and an inner confidence that comes from knowing you're loved and held.

6. Don't Walk Alone

If you can, walk through this devotional with a friend, spouse, or small group.
Sharing what you're learning breaks isolation and deepens growth.
Healing multiplies in community.

Each page of this devotional is a seed.
Plant it with honesty, water it with prayer,
and watch as God begins to grow peace where fear once lived.

By the end of these thirty days, you'll recognize something beautiful—the same love you once tried to control is now living freely within you. You don't have to have it all figured out before you begin.

Awareness is only the first step — healing happens in the time processing with the Holy Spirit. Each day of this devotional will help you recognize when fear is speaking and teach you how to respond from love instead of control.

As you move through these pages, don't analyze yourself too much. Let the Holy Spirit do the deeper work of revealing and restoring. These 30 days are not about fixing what's broken, but about *rediscovering who you are in the Father's love.*

So take a deep breath, invite Jesus into the process, and let's begin your journey *from fear to love but first a letter from your heavenly Father.*

💌 A Letter from the Father

Precious child,

Fear may be trauma's most paralyzing companion.
When you've been hurt, betrayed, or overwhelmed, fear moves in as a supposed protector —but it often becomes a prison warden, keeping you locked away from the very life and love you long for.

Trauma creates many forms of fear: fear of being hurt again, fear of trusting, fear of abandonment, fear of rejection, fear of intimacy, fear of failure, fear of success, and even fear of healing — because pain has become familiar. These fears build invisible walls around your heart, boundaries I never designed for you.

I want you to understand: **fear is not from Me.**
My Word says, *"I have not given you a spirit of fear, but of power, love, and a sound mind."* Fear comes from the enemy. It's designed to keep you small, isolated, and ineffective —to whisper that you must stay hidden to stay safe.

But here's what fear doesn't want you to know: **Courage isn't the absence of fear — it's feeling the fear and choosing faith anyway.**
Every time you choose to trust Me despite what you feel, you break fear's power over your life. Every time you take a trembling step forward, you prove that fear is no longer your master.

I am going to expose fear's lies and replace them with My truth.
Fear says, "You'll be hurt again."
I say, "I will protect and provide."
Fear says, "You can't handle this."
I say, "You can do all things through Christ who strengthens you."

A Prayer of Release From Fear

Father,
I come before You with an open heart. Fear has followed me for so
long — fear of being hurt, abandoned, rejected, unseen, unloved.
It crept in through pain and trauma, promising to protect me,
but it only built walls around my heart and kept me from the fullness
of Your love.

Today, I lay those fears at Your feet. I no longer want to live a life
limited by what frightens me. I renounce every spirit of fear that
entered through trauma —fear of abandonment, rejection, intimacy,
failure, even success. You did not give me a spirit of fear,
but of power, love, and a sound mind.

Forgive me, Lord, for letting fear make my decisions, for allowing it
to silence my faith, and for trusting safety more than surrender.
I confess that I've let fear shrink my dreams and build distance
between me and others. Please forgive me for every time I let fear
speak louder than Your voice.

Holy Spirit, come and fill every place fear once occupied. Expose
the lies that have whispered in my ear and replace them with the
truth of Your Word. Remind me that I am loved, chosen, and safe in
You. Teach me to walk by faith, even when my hands shake and my
heart trembles. Give me courage to take steps forward,
to trust You in uncertainty, and to live from love instead of fear.

Thank You for never leaving me alone in my healing.
Thank You that Your perfect love is driving out all fear,
and that You are making me whole again — heart, mind, and soul.

In Jesus' precious name,
Amen.

Day 1
The Battle Between Fear and Faith

"For God has not given us a spirit of fear, but of power and of love and of a sound mind."
— 2 Timothy 1:7

"You shall know the truth, and the truth shall make you free."
— John 8:32

Teaching

Fear is a quiet dictator.
It sits deep inside the human heart, whispering that safety depends on control.
When fear rules, love becomes conditional, relationships become battles, and peace disappears behind a wall of self-protection.

Some people express control loudly—through anger, commands, or intimidation.
Others express it silently—through withdrawal, guilt, or emotional distance.
Both are driven by the same root: *If I don't protect myself, I'll be hurt again.*

God never designed us to control love or steal it.
He designed us to **become love**—to let His presence flow through us like living water.
Love is secure because it comes from an unchanging Source.
The moment we try to grasp or manage it, it slips away, and fear takes the throne.

Every time you feel the need to dominate a conversation, prove yourself, or shut down emotionally, pause and notice the inner voice

saying, *"I must stay in charge."*
That voice is not the Holy Spirit; it's fear pretending to be wisdom.
Real wisdom begins with surrender, not strategy.

You may have learned control as a child—perhaps when trust was broken or affection felt unsafe.
The soul builds walls called *independence* or *perfectionism* to survive.
Those walls promise protection but end up becoming prisons.
The Lord wants to meet you there, in the very memory where control was born, and tell you the truth: **you are safe in Him**.

Healing doesn't come by will-power.
It comes by **truth**—the kind that cuts through the lies we built our lives around.
As Jesus said:

"You shall know the truth, and the truth shall make you free."

The truth reveals that fear has no legal right to stay once love moves in. Wherever you have tried to protect yourself, God invites you to trust His protection instead.
When you let go of control, you make room for the Holy Spirit to take over. And where the Spirit of the Lord is, there is liberty.

Selah — Pause and Ask:
"When did I first believe I had to protect myself instead of trusting God?"
Listen quietly. The Holy Spirit will bring memories to mind, not to shame you but to heal you.
Let Him show you that moment through His eyes.

Reflection Questions

1. In what situations do I feel the strongest need to stay in control?
2. What fear hides beneath that need? Rejection? Abandonment? Failure?
3. How might trusting God's love change the way I respond to people?

(Use the lines below to journal your thoughts.)

Prayer of Release

Father, in the name of Jesus, I renounce the spirit of fear and every lie that tells me I must control people or circumstances to be safe.
I lay down manipulation, anxiety, and self-protection.
Wash me in Your truth and fill me with perfect love that casts out fear. Teach me to rest in Your sovereignty.
Let Your peace rule in my heart and overflow to those around me.
Amen.

Deliverance Declaration

In the authority of Jesus Christ, I break every agreement with fear, control, and mistrust.
I command every spirit that feeds on anxiety and domination to leave my life now.
I receive the Spirit of love, power, and a sound mind.
My heart belongs fully to God.
I no longer live to control love—I live to become love.

Action Step

Today, before each significant interaction, pause and breathe deeply. Whisper: *"I am loved and secure in God."*
Then choose to listen with understanding rather than striving to be right. Peace will replace anxiety, and love will begin to flow freely again.

Day 2
Power That Protects

"Let all bitterness, wrath, anger, clamor, and evil speaking be put away from you, with all malice.
And be kind to one another, tenderhearted, forgiving one another, even as God in Christ forgave you."
— Ephesians 4:31-32

"The Lord will fight for you; you need only to be still."
— Exodus 14:14

Teaching

Anger often hides what words cannot confess—fear of rejection, fear of losing control, fear of being unseen.
When fear festers, it turns into the desire to **dominate**.
We shout, threaten, or manipulate not because we are strong, but because we are terrified of feeling weak.
That is not authority; it is bondage disguised as power.

True authority looks nothing like intimidation.
Jesus, the most powerful Man to walk the earth, washed His disciples' feet. He never ruled by force; He ruled by love.
Real strength is **gentleness anchored in truth**.

Emotional manipulation is one of the enemy's oldest tactics.
It twists love into leverage—using guilt, fear, or silence to control another's response. Scripture calls this a work of the flesh, and witchcraft not of the Spirit.
When someone uses affection as a reward or punishment, they are practicing **soulish control**, a subtle form of emotional witchcraft that seeks to bend another person's will through emotion instead of

yielding to God.
It can happen in homes, friendships, ministries, even marriages.
Where manipulation reigns, peace dies.

Perhaps you learned to survive through intimidation or learned helplessness.
You may have grown up watching adults use fear to gain obedience.
Without healing, that pattern repeats itself until someone decides, *It ends with me.*
Let today be that decision.

God's Spirit never pressures or shames.
He leads by conviction and truth, not by fear or guilt.
When you surrender your need to control, you step out of the counterfeit and into true power—the kind that protects, covers, and restores.

Healing from intimidation requires both repentance and recovery.
Repentance removes the counterfeit; recovery restores the heart.
Only a soul that has experienced unconditional love can stop demanding it from others.

"He who knows love, knows God"

Stillness is not weakness; it is confidence in the One who defends you. When you stop striving, God steps in.
When you release control, heaven releases peace.

Selah — Pause and Ask:
"When did I begin believing that anger would keep me safe?"
Invite the Holy Spirit to uncover the memory and bring His truth into that moment.

Reflection Questions

1. Do I use anger, sarcasm, or silence to make others back down?
2. What fear or wound am I protecting when I do that?
3. How can I replace intimidation with gentleness and truth today?

(Use the space below to journal your thoughts.)

_____
_____
_____
_____
_____
_____

Prayer of Renunciation

Lord Jesus, I confess that I have used anger, intimidation, or emotional pressure to feel safe or powerful.
Forgive me for wounding others through fear.
I renounce every pattern of manipulation, every agreement with control, and every trace of emotional witchcraft in my life.
Cleanse my heart, Lord, and teach me to walk in true authority—the kind that protects, not punishes.
Fill me with Your gentleness and strength.
Amen.

Deliverance Declaration

In the mighty name of Jesus Christ, I sever every soul-tie formed through fear, rage, or domination.
I break the power of guilt, manipulation, and intimidation.
Every spirit that feeds on anger or control has no place in me.

The peace of Christ now rules my heart.
I choose to walk in humility, compassion, and self-control.
My words will heal, not harm.
My presence will bring peace, not pressure.

Action Step

When you feel the rise of frustration or the urge to prove your point, pause for sixty seconds.
Breathe deeply and pray, *"Holy Spirit, fight for me while I stay still."*
Let the stillness disarm fear.
Choose a soft answer, and watch how the atmosphere changes.

Day 3
Breaking the Habit of Criticism

"Do not judge, or you too will be judged. For in the same way you judge others, you will be judged, and with the measure you use, it will be measured to you."
— Matthew 7:1-2

"Pleasant words are like a honeycomb, sweetness to the soul and health to the bones."
— Proverbs 16:24

Teaching

Criticism feels safe because it keeps the spotlight off our own pain.
It allows us to stay in control—analyzing, correcting, and measuring others instead of allowing God to measure us.
But judgment is a thief; it drains the heart of compassion and blinds us to our own need for grace.

When we constantly expose the faults of others, we are not protecting truth—we are protecting fear.
Fear of being unseen, fear of being wrong, fear of being insignificant.
So we talk, correct, and critique to feel powerful again.
Yet the moment we do, love leaves the room.

God never anointed our tongues to tear down.
He designed them to create life.
Every word spoken carries spiritual weight.
When we use words as weapons, we are participating in **emotional manipulation**—a form of control that silences others through shame or intimidation.
It is subtle, but it is destructive.

Perhaps you grew up in a home where love was earned by perfection and criticism was the language of control.
Without healing, that pattern follows us into adulthood, shaping how we parent, partner, and minister.
The Lord longs to break that cycle.
He wants to transform your voice from a weapon into a well—pouring refreshment instead of poison.

The enemy loves to twist discernment into suspicion and truth into accusation.
But the Holy Spirit convicts with kindness, not contempt.
When God reveals sin, His purpose is always restoration, never humiliation.
We must learn to do the same.

If your words have wounded, know this: He can redeem even your voice.
The same mouth that once cursed can now bless.
The same tongue that once criticized can now comfort.
Freedom begins the moment you admit, *"Lord, my words have been tools of control. Teach me to speak life."*

Healing from critical speech requires more than silence; it requires transformation.
As your heart softens, your speech will follow.
Ask God to make you a vessel of encouragement—a living echo of His mercy.

"Pleasant words are like a honeycomb, sweetness to the soul and health to the bones."

Let His sweetness replace the bitterness that has lived behind your lips.

Selah — Pause and Ask:
"Lord, what fear or pain makes me want to correct instead of connect?"
Wait for His gentle answer.
He will show you the root, and the truth will make you free.

Reflection Questions

1. Have my words been used to correct or to control?
2. What fear rises when I stop criticizing?
3. How would my relationships change if I spoke to build rather than to win?

(Use the space below to journal your thoughts.)

_____
_____
_____
_____
_____

Prayer of Healing and Cleansing

Father, I confess that I have used my words to control, to correct, and to protect my own insecurities.
Forgive me for wounding others with sarcasm, gossip, and judgment.
Wash my lips with the fire of Your altar.
Let my mouth speak only what edifies and brings grace to the hearer.
Replace criticism with compassion, and accusation with understanding.
Create in me a clean heart and renew a right spirit within me.
Amen.

Deliverance Declaration

In the name of Jesus Christ, I renounce the spirit of accusation, perfectionism, and pride.
I break every curse released through words of judgment, gossip, or condemnation.
I cancel their effect over my life and the lives of others.

I declare that my tongue belongs to the Lord.
From this day forward, my words will bring healing, not harm; blessing, not bondage.
I choose life, and I will speak life.

Action Step

Purposefully speak three affirming sentences today.
Bless the people you usually correct.
When you feel the urge to criticize, pause and whisper, *"Lord, teach me to love."*
Notice how peace fills the space where judgment once lived.

Day 4
Fear's Quiet Twin

"There is no fear in love; but perfect love casts out fear, because fear involves torment. But he who fears has not been made perfect in love."
— 1 John 4:18

"Whoever isolates himself seeks his own desire; he breaks out against all sound judgment."
— Proverbs 18:1

Teaching

Some people fight to stay in control by drawing near.
Others fight by pulling away.
The *distant* heart learns early that closeness feels dangerous, so it builds invisible walls.
Distance becomes safety; silence becomes armor.

Distance means physically or emotionally pulling away—avoiding eye contact, conversations, or closeness so you don't risk being hurt.
Silence means staying quiet inside even when you're physically present—keeping your thoughts or feelings locked up because speaking feels unsafe, confusing, or overwhelming.

Both distance and silence are ways the nervous system tries to keep you safe after pain.
They are not sins by themselves; they are *signals* that fear has taken the driver's seat.
The trouble begins when fear, not peace, starts deciding how long you stay hidden.

Perhaps you were told as a child that emotions were weakness, or you discovered that being honest brought rejection.
So you adapted.
You learned to survive by disappearing—smiling when needed, retreating when threatened.
No one could hurt you if they never truly knew you.
But the same wall that kept pain out also keeps love out.

God never designed your heart to live behind stone.
He made it soft enough to feel His presence and strong enough to withstand love's weight.
When you hide, you don't protect yourself; you simply disconnect from the One who heals.

Withdrawal is fear's quiet twin.
It whispers, *"I'm fine on my own."*
Yet deep down, loneliness testifies otherwise.
True safety isn't found in isolation but in intimacy with God.
He already knows every secret place within you—the walls, the fears, the memories—and He stands patiently at the gate saying, *"Let Me in."*

Jesus never forced anyone to open up, but He always invited.
He still does.
When you risk letting Him close, His love begins to touch the places that long ago went numb.
You start to feel again—peace, hope, joy.
And slowly, you realize that connection doesn't destroy you; it restores you.

Healing begins when you acknowledge that emotional distance is not peace—it's avoidance.
Peace comes when fear no longer dictates your boundaries.

"There is no fear in love; but perfect love casts out fear."

Let His perfect love enter the places you've hidden.
Walls built out of pain can only be torn down by grace.

Selah — Pause and Ask:
"Lord, where have I used silence or distance to protect myself? Show me the wound behind my wall, and teach me to trust You there."

Reflection Questions

1. When do I feel the need to withdraw or shut down?
2. What past experiences taught me that closeness equals danger?
3. How can I invite God—and safe people—into my heart again?

(Use the space below to journal your thoughts.)

\
\
\
\
\
\

Prayer of Surrender

Father, I confess that I have hidden behind emotional walls to protect myself from pain.
Forgive me for believing that isolation could keep me safe.
I open my heart to You today.
Heal the memories that taught me to fear connection.
Teach me how to love without fear and to trust without control.
I receive Your perfect love that casts out fear.
Amen.

Deliverance Declaration

In the name of Jesus Christ, I break agreement with fear, isolation, and emotional numbness.
Every spirit of withdrawal, rejection, and distrust has no place in my life.
I command the walls around my heart to come down in the power of the Cross.
I am free to feel, free to trust, and free to love.
The peace of God now guards my heart and mind in Christ Jesus.

Action Step

Reach out to someone you've quietly avoided.
Send a message, make a call, or simply pray for them.
Ask God to give you courage to connect without fear.
Each step toward openness invites more healing and more light.

Day 5
When Pain Becomes Power

"No, in all these things we are more than conquerors through Him who loved us."
— Romans 8:37

"The Lord is near to the brokenhearted and saves the crushed in spirit."
— Psalm 34:18

Teaching

Pain always looks for language.
If it can't find words, it finds roles—and one of the most deceptive roles pain can take is *the victim*.
It whispers, *"If I stay wounded, people will finally see me."*
And for a moment, sympathy feels like safety.

The victim posture doesn't mean you haven't truly suffered.
You have.
But when suffering becomes your identity, it slowly steals your strength.
The lie says, *"If I stop being the hurt one, I'll lose the attention that keeps me alive."*
But the truth says, *"You were never meant to live by pity; you were made to live by power."*

Sometimes we rehearse our pain because it's the only story we know.
We replay it in conversations and in our minds, hoping that if others finally understand, the ache will fade.
Yet the more we relive the wound, the deeper the roots of helplessness grow.

The enemy loves this cycle because it keeps your eyes on the injury instead of the Healer.

God never denies your pain; He dignifies it by redeeming it.
He takes what was used against you and turns it into a weapon of compassion.
But to receive that transformation, you must lay down the identity of *victim* and pick up the identity of *overcomer*.

There's a difference between processing pain and performing pain.
Processing leads to freedom; performing keeps you bound.
Performing says, *"If I stop hurting, I'll disappear."*
Processing says, *"I'm ready to be healed."*

Jesus understands every injustice you've faced.
He was betrayed, beaten, and abandoned—yet He never became bitter.
He didn't let pain define Him; He used it to redeem others.
The Cross proves that you can walk through suffering without letting it become your name.

The victim mindset often manipulates through guilt:
"If I'm miserable, someone will rescue me."
But no one can rescue what refuses to rise.
Your healing begins when you decide: *I will not live from my wound; I will live from His victory.*

"The Lord is near to the brokenhearted."
He draws close not to keep you broken, but to make you whole.
You are seen, valued, and strong—not because of what happened to you, but because of Who lives within you.

Selah — Pause and Ask:
"Lord, where have I used my pain to gain control or attention?
Show me how to release my story into Your hands so it can become testimony instead of identity."

Reflection Questions

1. When do I find comfort in sharing or reliving my pain?
2. Have I ever used my hurt to gain sympathy or avoid responsibility?
3. What would it look like to live as a conqueror instead of a victim?

(Use the space below to journal your thoughts.)

Prayer of Restoration

Father, You know every wound I've carried and every moment I felt unseen.
Forgive me for letting pain become my identity.
I choose today to lay down self-pity, resentment, and hopelessness.
Heal the places where trauma taught me to depend on attention instead of Your presence.
Fill me with courage to rise and take my place as Your child—strong, loved, and free.
Amen.

Deliverance Declaration

In the name of Jesus Christ, I renounce the spirit of victimhood, self-pity, and despair.

I break agreement with every lie that says I am powerless or forgotten.
I command every stronghold of shame, guilt, and manipulation to leave me now.
I receive the Spirit of adoption, strength, and victory.
I am no longer defined by what was done to me; I am defined by what Christ has done for me.
I rise in His power as more than a conqueror.

Action Step

Write a short letter to your past self—the one who was hurt.
Speak to that version of you with kindness:
"You are safe now. You are not alone. God is healing you."
Then pray, thanking God for turning pain into purpose.
Choose one small act of service today; helping someone else breaks the victim cycle and activates compassion instead of control.

Day 6
Energy Draining People

"Do two walk together unless they have agreed to do so?"
— Amos 3:3

"Do not be deceived: 'Bad company corrupts good morals.'"
— 1 Corinthians 15:33

"Pursue peace with all people, and holiness, without which no one will see the Lord."
— Hebrews 12:14

Teaching

Every relationship is an exchange of words, emotions, and spiritual atmosphere.
When both hearts are grounded in God, that exchange feels peaceful—each person leaves encouraged, strengthened, and seen.
But when fear, manipulation, or unhealed wounds drive one side, the exchange becomes heavy, confusing, or draining.
That heaviness is not "too much empathy." It is your spirit recognizing an *unequal yoke*.

Toxic exchanges are not always loud or dramatic.
Sometimes they come as constant crisis, subtle guilt, or quiet control.
You walk away feeling smaller, guilty, or anxious, even though you can't explain why.
This isn't judgment—it's discernment.
The Holy Spirit inside you is alerting you that something in the flow of love has been replaced by striving or fear.

Healthy love flows freely; unhealthy love demands payment.
When someone expects you to rescue, fix, or carry what only God can heal, you step out of grace and into emotional bondage.
The Lord never called you to be anyone's savior—that role belongs to Jesus alone.
You can care deeply without becoming captive to another's chaos.

This awareness matters because manipulation often hides behind care.
What begins as compassion can turn into control when one person feeds on the attention or energy of another.
If you constantly leave a conversation feeling responsible for someone's emotions, you may be trapped in a *toxic exchange*.

Discernment does not mean withdrawal from everyone who struggles.
It means recognizing where grace ends and control begins.
Love never enables sin or codependency; it empowers truth.
When you recognize a pattern that continually steals peace, the answer is not accusation—it's boundaries.
Boundaries are not punishment; they are protection for both hearts.

Ask the Holy Spirit to teach you the rhythm of relational peace.
He will show you when to comfort, when to confront, and when to step back.
Remember: even Jesus sometimes withdrew to pray.
He loved everyone yet was not controlled by anyone.

"Pursue peace with all people."
You cannot control whether others choose peace—but you can guard the peace within you.

Selah — Pause and Ask:
"Lord, which relationships strengthen my walk with You, and which ones constantly drain my spirit?
Teach me how to stay loving without losing myself."

Reflection Questions

1. Who or what consistently leaves me feeling guilty, anxious, or small?
2. Do I confuse enabling with compassion?
3. How can I love people without taking responsibility for their emotions or choices?

(Use the space below to journal your thoughts.)

Prayer for Discernment and Peace

Father, give me eyes to see relationships as You see them.
Expose every unhealthy exchange where fear, guilt, or manipulation has taken root.
Forgive me for confusing control with compassion.
Teach me how to set boundaries that honor You and protect the peace You've given me.
Fill every empty place with Your love so that I no longer draw or drain others out of fear.
Let my connections flow with purity, truth, and grace.
Amen.

Deliverance Declaration

In the name of Jesus Christ, I renounce every soul-tie and every emotional entanglement rooted in fear, shame, or manipulation.
I break the power of toxic dependence and release every person I have tried to carry in my own strength.
I receive the freedom of the Holy Spirit to love without bondage and to give without depletion.
My relationships are governed by peace and truth, not fear and control.
The Lord restores balance, purity, and rest to my heart.

Action Step

Choose one boundary today that protects your peace—whether it's pausing before replying to a draining message, saying *no* with kindness, or spending quiet time with God before helping others. Every healthy boundary invites love to flow freely again.

Day 7
Name That Drama

"Search me, O God, and know my heart; try me and know my anxious thoughts.
See if there is any wicked way in me, and lead me in the way everlasting."
— Psalm 139:23–24

"And you shall know the truth, and the truth shall make you free."
— John 8:32

"Therefore confess your sins to each other and pray for each other so that you may be healed.
The prayer of a righteous person is powerful and effective."
— James 5:16

Teaching

Denial is a quiet deceiver.
It hides behind good intentions and religious language, convincing us that things are "not that bad."
But healing never comes to what we refuse to name.
Freedom begins when we finally say, *"This is what's been happening, and I want it to change."*

Naming the drama doesn't mean exposing others—it means allowing the Holy Spirit to expose *you*.
It is choosing truth over comfort.
When you name a pattern—control, manipulation, silence, fear, criticism—it loses power.
What remains hidden controls you; what's confessed loses authority.

Awareness is not condemnation; it is invitation.
God never reveals to embarrass—He reveals to restore.
His light doesn't shame; it heals.
When you allow the Lord to show you how fear has shaped your behavior, that's not failure; that's freedom beginning.

Sometimes we can't see the patterns we live in because they've always been there.
Control may feel normal; guilt may feel like love.
But when peace becomes rare, that's your clue that something unseen is ruling.
Ask the Holy Spirit to be your mirror.
He will show you without harshness—never condemning, only convicting.

It's not enough to recognize what's wrong; we must also take responsibility for our part.
Accountability is love in action.
When you admit your patterns to God—and, when safe, to a trusted believer—you remove shame's last hiding place.
What was once a secret becomes a testimony in progress.

"Confess your sins to one another and pray for one another, that you may be healed."
Healing doesn't come through isolation; it comes through humility.

Accountability is not about punishment; it's about partnership with grace.
It's saying, *"I can't walk this out alone, but I don't have to."*
The Lord often uses honest friends, pastors, counselors, or mentors as mirrors of mercy—people who help us stay aware when old habits try to return.

If you've been afraid to face your own control dramas—fear of rejection, guilt, or loss of image—remember:
God already knows.
You're not revealing something new; you're agreeing with truth.
And truth always makes you free.

Selah — Pause and Ask:
"Holy Spirit, show me the patterns I've hidden from myself.
Help me see the moments I justified control or avoided honesty.
Teach me to welcome Your correction as love."

Reflection Questions

1. What behaviors or attitudes do I most often minimize or excuse?
2. Is there someone safe I can share honestly with about what I'm learning?
3. How do I respond when God or others lovingly confront me?

(Use the space below to journal your thoughts.)

Prayer of Honesty and Surrender

Father, I invite Your light into every corner of my heart.
Search me and reveal what I've hidden—my fear, my control, my pride.
I choose to stop defending what hurts me.
Forgive me for protecting my image more than my integrity.
Teach me to walk in truth without shame.
Surround me with people who love me enough to hold me accountable and pray me through to freedom.
Amen.

Deliverance Declaration

In the name of Jesus Christ, I renounce denial, deception, and every false comfort that keeps me bound.
I break agreement with shame and secrecy.
Every lie that says I must hide is broken now by the blood of Jesus.
I receive the Spirit of truth, clarity, and boldness.
I walk in the light as He is in the light, and the truth sets me free.

Action Step

Choose one area where you've been afraid to be honest—with God, with yourself, or with someone else.
Write it down, pray over it, and if safe, share it with a trusted believer or mentor.
Light weakens shame, and confession opens the door to healing.

Day 8
Repentance as Freedom

"If we confess our sins, He is faithful and just to forgive us our sins and to cleanse us from all unrighteousness."
— 1 John 1:9

"He who conceals his sins does not prosper, but whoever confesses and forsakes them finds mercy."
— Proverbs 28:13

"The kindness of God leads you to repentance."
— Romans 2:4

Teaching

Repentance has often been misunderstood as humiliation or punishment, but in God's kingdom it is an act of **love and liberation**.
It is not groveling before an angry Judge—it is returning to a gentle Father who already knows what went wrong and still wants you home.

When we first become aware of our patterns—control, manipulation, withdrawal, fear, criticism—our hearts can feel heavy.
Shame may whisper, *"You'll never change."*
But repentance answers, *"I'm changing right now."*
Repentance is movement—from darkness into light, from pride into peace.

Confession is not simply naming what happened; it's releasing ownership of it.
It's saying, *"This no longer belongs to me; it belongs to the Cross."*

Every time you confess, you open a window in the soul, and the breath of God rushes in.

Some people fear confession because they associate it with exposure.
But exposure in God's hands is healing, not humiliation.
When He shines light, He does so as a physician, not a prosecutor.
He reveals only to restore.
To confess, then, is to cooperate with the Healer's touch.

Repentance also awakens **compassion**—for ourselves and for others.
When we see our own brokenness honestly, we stop expecting perfection from anyone else.
Grace softens us.
We become gentler, less defensive, and more aware of how easily we all drift from truth when we forget love.

"The kindness of God leads you to repentance."

Notice—it is *kindness*, not fear, that turns the heart.
True repentance isn't driven by dread of punishment; it's drawn by the beauty of mercy.
The more you see how tenderly God forgives, the less you want to cling to what hurt you.

Repentance is not a one-time event; it's a rhythm of renewal.
Just as you breathe in and out, you confess and receive grace—daily, continually.
It keeps the heart clean and the conscience soft.

If you've avoided confession because you fear rejection, hear this truth:
You cannot disappoint the God who already knows everything about you and still chose to love you completely.
When you finally let go, peace comes rushing in like air to a suffocating room.

Selah — Pause and Ask:
"Lord, what do You want me to bring into the light today?
Show me not just what I've done, but what You want to heal."

Reflection Questions

1. What area of my life have I kept hidden out of fear or shame?
2. When I confess to God, what emotions surface—relief, fear, resistance?
3. How has God's kindness invited me to change without condemnation?

(Use the space below to journal your thoughts.)

Prayer of Repentance and Renewal

Father, I come into Your light without excuse or defense.
I confess the ways I have controlled, feared, and hidden from truth.
Thank You that Your mercy is greater than my mistakes.
Wash me clean, Lord, and renew a right spirit within me.
Replace shame with peace, guilt with gratitude, and fear with freedom.
Teach me to live each day in humble awareness of Your grace.
Amen.

Deliverance Declaration

In the name of Jesus Christ, I renounce shame, self-condemnation, and every spirit that resists repentance.
I break agreement with guilt, denial, and pride.
I declare that my heart is open and my conscience purified by the blood of Jesus.

I am not defined by my past but renewed by His mercy.
The Spirit of truth reigns in me, and I walk freely in grace.

Action Step

Set aside a quiet moment today to write out a personal confession between you and God.
List anything that burdens your heart—words, actions, fears, or attitudes—and then read 1 John 1:9 aloud.
Afterward, tear up or safely discard the paper as a prophetic act of release.
Breathe deeply and thank Him for forgiveness that is final.

Day 9
Walking in the Light

**"But if we walk in the light as He is in the light, we have fellowship with one another,
and the blood of Jesus Christ His Son cleanses us from all sin."**
— 1 John 1:7

"You will keep him in perfect peace, whose mind is stayed on You, because he trusts in You."
— Isaiah 26:3

**"Be sober, be vigilant; because your adversary the devil walks about like a roaring lion,
seeking whom he may devour."**
— 1 Peter 5:8

Teaching

Freedom is not a single moment—it's a lifestyle of awareness.
Once the light of truth has touched your heart, the next step is learning to stay there.
Awareness means living awake to the whispers of the Holy Spirit, alert to peace, and quick to notice when fear or pride try to slip back in.

The enemy's greatest tactic is not always temptation; often it is distraction.
He tries to dull your awareness with busyness, worry, or emotional noise so that you forget who you are and what you've been set free from.
That's why Scripture tells us to *be sober and vigilant*—not fearful, but awake.

Walking in the light means inviting God into every part of your day, not just the sacred moments.
It's noticing His presence while you work, parent, create, or rest.
It's asking, *"What's happening in my heart right now?"* before reacting.
This simple awareness keeps you from falling back into old control dramas.

When you sense tension or anxiety rising, don't shame yourself—**pause and invite truth**.
Ask, *"Lord, what's happening inside me? What am I afraid of losing?"*
Awareness doesn't condemn; it clarifies.
The more you practice it, the quicker you recognize when peace has left the room—and the faster you can return to it.

Awareness is not overthinking; it's spiritual attentiveness.
Overthinking is fear trying to control every outcome.
Awareness is love listening for God's voice in the present moment.

"You will keep him in perfect peace, whose mind is stayed on You."

Peace doesn't come from perfection; it comes from focus.
When your mind stays on Christ—His promises, His love, His nearness—fear loses its grip.
The Holy Spirit becomes your daily mirror, gently showing you when your thoughts wander and guiding you back to truth.

Freedom grows in the soil of awareness.
When you know the truth, you notice deception faster.
When you stay tender before God, you catch resentment before it hardens. When you walk in gratitude, offense can't take root.
Awareness isn't about paranoia; it's about partnership with the Holy Spirit.

He is not waiting for you to fail—He's walking with you to succeed.
If you stumble, awareness helps you rise quickly, shake off shame, and return to grace.

Selah — Pause and Ask:
"Holy Spirit, help me notice the moments when I start to lose peace. Show me how to stay aware of Your presence all day long."

Reflection Questions

1. What situations most often cause me to lose awareness of God's peace?
2. How does the Holy Spirit usually alert me when something is off?
3. What simple practices help me stay present and grounded in truth?

(Use the space below to journal your thoughts.)

_____
_____
_____
_____
_____
_____

Prayer of Awareness and Peace

Father, thank You for the light of truth that has set me free.
Teach me how to remain awake to Your presence throughout my day.
When I feel fear, frustration, or pride rising, remind me to stop and listen for Your voice.
Keep my mind steady and my heart soft.
Let Your peace become the atmosphere of my soul.
Amen.

Deliverance Declaration

In the name of Jesus Christ, I close every door to distraction, deception, and fear.
I break agreement with spiritual blindness and emotional numbness.
My eyes are open, and my heart is alert to the truth.
I walk in the light as He is in the light, and His peace rules my thoughts.
The blood of Jesus cleanses me daily, and I am fully awake to His love.

Action Step

Take five minutes today to be still in silence.
Close your eyes, breathe deeply, and say: *"Lord, make me aware of You."*
Don't rush the moment.
Just notice His peace.
Every time you practice awareness, you strengthen your ability to live free.

Day 10
Restored Connection

"Be kind and compassionate to one another, forgiving each other, just as in Christ God forgave you."
— Ephesians 4:32

"Blessed are the pure in heart, for they shall see God."
— Matthew 5:8

"Above all, love each other deeply, because love covers a multitude of sins."
— 1 Peter 4:8

Teaching

When awareness matures, it becomes compassion.
Once you've faced the truth about your own patterns and fears, you begin to see other people through gentler eyes.
You realize that the ones who hurt you were often just as afraid as you were.
This doesn't excuse wrong behavior, but it explains the brokenness behind it—and that understanding becomes the seed of forgiveness.

True compassion grows out of clarity, not denial.
It does not pretend that evil is good or that pain didn't happen; it simply refuses to let bitterness write the final chapter.
When you forgive, you are not saying, *"What you did was okay."*
You are saying, *"What you did will not control me anymore."*

Restored connection begins inside you.
Before you can reconnect with others, you must reconnect with God and yourself.
If shame has kept you withdrawn, let His mercy draw you close

again.
When you see yourself through the Father's eyes—beloved, chosen, capable—you stop relating to people through fear and start relating through love.

"Be kind and compassionate to one another, forgiving each other."

Kindness is not weakness; it is strength under grace.
Compassion does not mean re-entering toxic situations, but it does mean releasing the grip of resentment.
Forgiveness is the act of freeing your own heart so God can fill it again.

Many people think that once they set boundaries or walk away from a controlling relationship, they are done.
But closure doesn't come from distance alone; it comes from forgiveness.
Without forgiveness, distance simply becomes another wall.
Forgiveness tears the wall down from *your* side so you can breathe again.

Purity of heart is not perfection; it is clarity—seeing people as God sees them, without the fog of offense.
When your heart is clean, your discernment becomes sharp.
You can love without losing yourself and see without condemning.

Ask God to help you live from that clear space where compassion and truth hold hands.
That is where freedom matures.
The light that once exposed now guides.
The same awareness that once felt painful now becomes peaceful.

Selah — Pause and Ask:
"Lord, who do I still need to forgive?
Where has resentment or disappointment dimmed my clarity?
Show me how to see others through Your mercy."

Reflection Questions

1. Who do I still carry in my heart with resentment, fear, or guilt?
2. How can I forgive without reopening old wounds or unhealthy ties?
3. What does restored connection with God, myself, and others look like for me?

(Use the space below to journal your thoughts.)

_____
_____
_____
_____
_____
_____

Prayer of Restoration and Forgiveness

Father, thank You for the light that has exposed truth and the mercy that covers sin.
I bring before You every person who has hurt or controlled me, and every person I have hurt or tried to control.
I choose forgiveness—not because they deserve it, but because You have forgiven me.
Heal my heart from bitterness and teach me to walk in compassion without compromise.
Restore peace to every part of my story.
Amen.

_____

Deliverance Declaration

In the name of Jesus Christ, I renounce unforgiveness, bitterness, and resentment.
I break the power of emotional attachment to past pain and declare freedom from every soul-tie rooted in anger or regret.
I receive the cleansing of the blood of Jesus and the renewing of my mind by the Holy Spirit.
My heart is pure, my conscience clear, and my relationships covered by grace.
I walk in love, truth, and compassion.

Action Step

Write the names of those you need to forgive.
Beside each name, pray: *"Lord, I release them to You."*
Then, thank God for the peace that comes with clarity.
End your day by reading Matthew 5:8 and whispering: *"Blessed are the pure in heart."*

Day 11
From Control to Godfidence

"Blessed is the man who trusts in the Lord, whose confidence is in Him."
— Jeremiah 17:7

"So do not throw away your confidence; it will be richly rewarded.
You need to persevere so that when you have done the will of God, you will receive what He has promised."
— Hebrews 10:35-36

"The Lord will be your confidence and will keep your foot from being caught."
— Proverbs 3:26

Control is a counterfeit version of trust.
It promises safety but produces exhaustion.
We grasp for outcomes because deep down we doubt that anyone—even God—will hold things together if we let go.
We think, *"If I just manage everything right, I'll finally feel secure."*
But control is a fragile throne; one small change and it crumbles.
Healing begins when we release that fear and rediscover the truth:
God is in control of the outcome. He is God and we are not.

When we trust Him, control loses its purpose.
We no longer need to manipulate, predict, or strive.
Our hearts shift from panic to peace.
That shift is called Godfidence—a steady assurance rooted in who God is, not in who we are.

Godfidence is not pride.
Pride says, *"I can handle this on my own."*
Godfidence says, *"I can face this because God is with me."*
Pride exalts the self; Godfidence exalts God.

Pride closes its ears; Godfidence listens.
Pride takes credit; Godfidence gives glory.

Worldly confidence says, *"I've got this."*
Godfidence says, *"God's got me."*
One builds on ego; the other rests on surrender.
Pride pushes to prove itself; Godfidence moves in quiet power.

Godfidence grows in the soil of surrender.
Every time you release the need to control, you make room for faith to rise.
You stop asking, *"What if everything goes wrong?"* and start declaring, *"Even if it does, God will still be faithful."*

When fear loses its grip, trust takes its place.
This is not the absence of weakness—it's the awareness that His strength overcomes your weakness.
Paul said, *"When I am weak, then I am strong."*
That paradox defines Godfidence: humility anchored in divine reliability.

Many believers confuse humility with self-doubt, but humility is not thinking less of yourself—it's thinking of yourself less.
It's shifting focus from your limitations to God's limitless ability.
When your gaze turns upward, anxiety loses oxygen.
Control no longer feels necessary, because God has proven Himself faithful.

"The Lord will be your confidence and will keep your foot from being caught."

Let that promise settle into your spirit: *The Lord Himself will be your confidence.*
He will steady your steps, provide wisdom, and open doors you could never force.
You don't have to hold everything together; you only have to hold onto Him.

Godfidence empowers you to act without fear, speak without pride, and rest without worry.
It replaces striving with steady faith.
It doesn't shout; it stands.
And because its foundation is God's character, not personal success, it cannot be shaken.

Selah — Pause and Ask:
"Lord, where am I still depending on my own strength instead of trusting Yours?
Teach me to exchange my control for Your peace, my fear for Your faithfulness."

Reflection Questions

1. In what areas of my life do I still rely on control instead of trust?
2. How does it feel different when I act from peace instead of pride?
3. What would living with Godfidence look like in my daily choices?

(Use the space below to journal your thoughts.)

Prayer of Trust and Exchange

Father, I release every false confidence I have built—my control, my perfectionism, my fear of failure.
I confess that I have relied on my own strength more than Your Spirit.
I receive today the gift of Godfidence: faith that rests in Your character, not my performance.
Teach me to walk in quiet boldness, knowing that You go before me and keep me steady.
Replace every anxious thought with trust and every self-reliant plan with surrender.
Amen.

Deliverance Declaration

In the name of Jesus Christ, I break agreement with pride, fear, and the need to control outcomes.
I renounce the lie that I must hold everything together to be safe.
The Lord is my confidence, my provider, and my defender.
I stand firm, not in myself, but in the power of His Spirit.
I am rooted, secure, and unshakable because God is faithful.

Action Step

When you face a decision today, stop and pray first.
Say out loud, *"God, I trust You with this."*
Then act from peace, not pressure.
Each time you do, you are strengthening your Godfidence and loosening fear's hold on your heart.

Day 12
Staying Connected

"I am the vine; you are the branches.
Whoever stays connected to Me, and I to him, will bear much fruit; apart from Me you can do nothing."
— John 15:5

"Come to Me, all you who are weary and pushing yourselves to the limit, and I will give you rest."
— Matthew 11:28 (adapted)

"Be still, and know that I am God."
— Psalm 46:10

Teaching

There's a kind of exhaustion that coffee can't fix.
It's the tired that lives under your skin—the kind that comes from *always* having to make things happen.
That's what happens when you live **running on empty**—chasing peace instead of receiving it.

Jesus offered us a different rhythm: *"Stay connected to Me."*
He never asked us to impress Him with productivity.
He simply invited us to do life *with* Him, not *for* Him.

When you're **pushing yourself to the limit**, every moment feels urgent.
You overthink, over-plan, and over-commit, hoping it will finally feel "enough."
But pressure steals peace.
And when peace leaves, so does clarity.

Staying connected looks completely different.
It's not laziness—it's alignment.
It means you move through your day aware of God's presence in small things:
breathing before answering, pausing before reacting, remembering you're loved before proving yourself.

You can still work hard, dream big, and show up fully—just not alone.
When your heart stays connected, the weight shifts from your shoulders to His.
You stop performing for approval and start partnering with grace.

Running on empty says, *"If I don't handle it, it will all fall apart."*
Staying connected says, *"God's got this, and He's leading me one step at a time."*
One burns you out; the other fills you up.

"Come to Me, all you who are weary."
Jesus isn't talking only to the overworked; He's calling to the over-responsible—the ones trying to fix everything and everyone.
His rest isn't the absence of work; it's the presence of peace.

When you live this way, fruit—the good stuff like joy, patience, and kindness—shows up naturally.
You don't have to force it; it grows from connection.
And when storms come, you stay steady because your roots run deep.

Selah — Pause and Ask:
"Lord, where have I been running on empty?
What would it look like today to slow down and stay connected to You?"

Reflection Questions

1. Where in my life am I pushing too hard or trying to make things happen?
2. What helps me notice when I'm disconnected from God's peace?
3. How can I start doing life *with* God instead of *for* Him?

(Use the space below to journal your thoughts.)

Prayer of Rest and Realignment

Father, I'm tired of carrying what was never mine.
I've been running on empty—trying to control, fix, and prove.
Today I choose to slow down.
Teach me how to stay connected to You in every moment.
Remind me that Your love isn't earned; it's received.
Fill me with Your peace where pressure once lived.
Let Your presence be my pace.
Amen.

Deliverance Declaration

In the name of Jesus Christ, I break agreement with striving, burnout, and self-reliance.
I renounce the lie that my value comes from what I achieve.
I am rooted in Christ, the Vine; His life flows through me.
I will not run on empty—I will live filled.
The peace of God replaces pressure, and grace carries me forward.

Action Step

Take a five-minute pause during your busiest part of the day.
Turn off notifications, close your eyes, and breathe slowly.
Whisper: *"God, I'm here. Let's do this together."*
Notice how the atmosphere shifts.
That's staying connected—doing life with God, not for God.

Day 13
Filling the Empty Places

"The Lord will guide you continually, and satisfy your soul in drought,
and strengthen your bones; you shall be like a watered garden, and like a spring of water, whose waters do not fail."
— Isaiah 58:11

"My grace is sufficient for you, for My strength is made perfect in weakness."
— 2 Corinthians 12:9

"You open Your hand and satisfy the desire of every living thing."
— Psalm 145:16

Teaching

When you finally slow down after years of running, you may feel an unexpected ache inside—a quiet emptiness that used to be hidden beneath the noise and productivity. We ache because deep down we crave communion with the Father. Don't be afraid of that quiet space.
That emptiness is not there to torment you; it's an invitation to come to Him.

Many of us try to fill that space with activity, people, or validation. We scroll, we plan, we overthink, anything to avoid the stillness. But every distraction is just a substitute for what our souls really crave: the loving presence of our Father.

Only He can fill the empty places with something that actually lasts.

It's easy to confuse being *busy* with being *filled.*
But busyness only masks emptiness for a moment.
The truth is, you can be surrounded by people and still feel alone, or appear strong while quietly breaking inside.
The good news is that the Holy Spirit doesn't fill perfect people; He fills *available* ones.
He's not waiting for you to be fixed—He's waiting for you to be honest.

"My grace is sufficient for you, for My strength is made perfect in weakness."

When you allow God into your weakness, He doesn't shame it—He inhabits it.
He turns emptiness into capacity.
He takes what used to be a wound and makes it a well.

Letting Him fill your empty places means being still long enough to notice what's missing:
the peace you traded for control, the joy you gave up to survive, the dreams you buried to stay safe.
He remembers them all, and He's ready to breathe life into them again.

Sometimes the Holy Spirit will gently bring up old pain so He can pour comfort where fear used to live.
Other times, He'll highlight the subtle ways you've been self-protecting so He can teach you to rest in His protection instead.
Healing doesn't rush; it receives.

God never fills a space you refuse to open.
But when you open your hands—even trembling ones—He moves in quietly, faithfully, completely.
What once felt like emptiness becomes overflow.

Selah — Pause and Ask:
"God, what space in me have I kept closed to you?
What part of my heart feels empty or numb?
Fill that place with Your love until nothing else fits there."

Reflection Questions

1. What do I reach for when I start to feel empty or lonely?
2. Where in my life do I still sense a lack of peace or joy?
3. How can I make space today for God to fill what I've been trying to fix?

(Use the space below to journal your thoughts.)

Prayer of Filling and Wholeness

Father, You see every empty space inside me—the quiet loneliness, the fears I can't explain, the areas I've kept hidden.
I open my heart to You now.
Fill me with Your presence where emptiness has lived.
Replace anxiety with peace, regret with hope, and striving with rest.
Thank You that Your grace is enough and that Your strength shows up right where I feel weakest.
Let Your fullness flow through every part of me until my life becomes a reflection of Your love.
Amen.

Deliverance Declaration

In the name of Jesus Christ, I renounce emptiness, loneliness, and every lie that tells me I am incomplete.
I break agreement with false comfort and quick fixes.
I declare that I am a dwelling place of the Holy Spirit, and He fills me to overflowing.
I will not live running on empty—I will live filled with His peace, power, and joy.
The Lord satisfies my soul, and nothing else will take His place.

Action Step

Find a quiet spot today—maybe in your car, your backyard, or a corner of your home.
Take three deep breaths and imagine handing your empty places to God.
Say aloud: *"Lord, here's the space that feels empty. Fill it with You."*
Stay there a moment and notice the peace that begins to settle in. That's what being filled feels like.

Day 14
Letting Go of the False Self

"You were taught, with regard to your former way of life, to put off your old self,
which is being corrupted by its deceitful desires;
to be made new in the attitude of your minds;
and to put on the new self, created to be like God in true righteousness and holiness."
— Ephesians 4:22-24

"The Lord does not look at the things people look at.
People look at the outward appearance, but the Lord looks at the heart."
— 1 Samuel 16:7

"Where the Spirit of the Lord is, there is freedom."
— 2 Corinthians 3:17

Teaching

At some point in life, many of us become someone we were never meant to be.
We shape-shift to survive—becoming the strong one, the funny one, the quiet one, the fixer, the peacekeeper.
We learn roles to earn belonging, and somewhere along the way, we start to believe that role *is* who we are.

But those versions of ourselves—the ones built out of fear, performance, or pain—are not the real you.
They are survival strategies, not identities.

Maybe you had to grow up too fast, carry too much, or pretend you didn't care when you did.

Maybe you learned that being invisible was safer than being honest.
The *false self* forms around those moments like armor—helpful at first, but heavy over time.
What once protected you begins to imprison you.

God isn't asking you to throw away your personality; He's asking to heal your *identity*.
He wants to strip away the layers you built to be loved so that your real self—the one He designed—can finally breathe.

"Even before He made the world, God loved us and chose us in Christ to be holy, whole, and blameless in His love.
He decided in advance to bring us into His own family through Jesus Christ.
This is what He wanted to do, and it made Him glad."
— Ephesians 1:4-6 (modern paraphrase)

You were **chosen before you were broken**.
Your worth isn't something you earn—it's something God decided long before your story began.
You don't have to fight for belonging; you already *belong to the Beloved*.
God didn't just accept you reluctantly; He delighted to call you His own.
You were called to live holy and whole, surrounded by love, not driven by fear.
When that truth takes root, the false self loses its purpose.

Letting go of who you had to be is not betrayal—it's redemption.
You're not abandoning the strong, helpful, or responsible parts of you; you're letting them be healed by love instead of driven by survival.
The world teaches us to "reinvent ourselves," but God calls us to *return* to ourselves—to the person He imagined before the pain and the pretending.

That's what real freedom looks like: not becoming someone new, but remembering who you've always been in His eyes.

Selah — Pause and Ask:
"God, what parts of me were built on fear or survival?
Show me the real me underneath the armor."

Reflection Questions

1. What version of myself have I used to feel safe or accepted?
2. When did I first believe I had to be that person to be loved?
3. What would it look like to let God love the *real* me—the one under all the layers?

(Use the space below to journal your thoughts.)

Prayer of Release and Reconnection

Father, thank You for loving me beyond every mask I've worn.
I confess that I've lived from fear instead of truth, from performance instead of peace. Today I choose to release the false identities I built to survive. Show me who I am in You—whole, chosen, and deeply loved. Heal the memories that shaped my false self and breathe life into the real me You designed.
Amen.

Deliverance Declaration

In the name of Jesus Christ, I renounce every false identity and every mask I've used to feel safe or worthy.
I break agreement with shame, fear, perfectionism, and performance.
I am not who trauma made me; I am who God created me to be.
I put off the old self and put on the new, clothed in righteousness and peace.
I am part of the Beloved, holy and whole in His love.
Where His Spirit is, there is freedom—and that freedom is mine.

Action Step

Stand in front of a mirror today—not to critique, but to reconnect.
Look yourself in the eyes and say:
"I am chosen. I am loved. I am part of the Beloved. I am free to be me."
Let those words settle deep inside until they start to feel true.
Because they are.

Day 15
Trading lies for God's Truth

"Do not be conformed to the pattern of this world,
but be transformed by the renewing of your mind.
Then you will be able to test and approve what God's will is—
His good, pleasing, and perfect will."
— Romans 12:2

"We take captive every thought to make it obedient to Christ."
— 2 Corinthians 10:5

"You will know the truth, and the truth will make you free."
— John 8:32

Teaching

Freedom starts in the mind long before it shows up anywhere else.
Even after you've been set free in your spirit, your thoughts may still speak the old language of fear, rejection, or control.
That's why Scripture tells us not just to believe differently—but to *think* differently.

Renewing your mind is not about forcing yourself to think happy thoughts.
It's about learning to recognize lies, uproot them, and replace them with God's truth until peace becomes your new normal.

Think of your mind like a garden.
Every thought is a seed.
If you plant words of worry, self-criticism, or hopelessness, those roots grow fast—and they choke out joy.
But when you plant truth, grace, and gratitude, peace begins to bloom where fear once lived.

Many of our thoughts are leftovers from old seasons—memories of who we *used* to be or how others treated us.
They sound familiar, but they're not factual.
You might catch yourself thinking things like:

- "I'll always mess things up."
- "No one really understands me."
- "If I don't stay in control, everything will fall apart."
- **"I'm a failure, and God must be disappointed in me."**

That last one—**the lie about failure**—is one of the enemy's favorites.
It convinces you that your mistakes define you, when God says your response to them refines you.
Failure doesn't disqualify you; it reveals where you're learning to lean on grace.
In God's kingdom, falling is not final—it's part of growing.
Every time you rise again, you prove the power of redemption.

God never speaks to you through shame, fear, or panic.
His voice always carries peace, even when He's correcting you.
He doesn't label you by your past; He calls you by your purpose.

"Do not be conformed to the pattern of this world, but be transformed by the renewing of your mind."

Renewing means there's a *new way to think* available—one that reflects heaven, not hurt.
When you replace old lies with God's promises, you're not pretending; you're practicing truth until it becomes instinct.

This isn't instant.
It's daily—sometimes moment by moment.
But every time you stop a negative thought and speak God's truth instead, you're rewiring your mind for freedom.
Over time, peace becomes your first reaction, not fear.

Renewing your mind is how you keep your healing.
Without it, the heart drifts back to old habits.

But with it, you begin to walk in consistent victory—not by effort, but by awareness.

This process is not willpower; it's partnership.
You bring your thoughts; God brings His truth.
Together, you build a new mindset grounded in love.

Selah — Pause and Ask:
"Lord, what thought patterns have been running my life?
Which ones sound like fear instead of faith?
Show me Your truth in their place."

Reflection Questions

1. What negative thought keeps looping in my mind most often?
2. What truth from Scripture can I replace it with?
3. How can I make space in my day to pause and check what I'm thinking before I react?

(Use the space below to journal your thoughts.)

Prayer for a Renewed Mind

Father, thank You for giving me a sound mind and the ability to think with peace.
I surrender every thought that doesn't line up with Your truth.
I give You my fear of failure, my self-criticism, and every lie that says I'll never be enough.
Teach me to see failure the way You do—as an opportunity to grow in grace.
Where fear once ruled, let faith rise.
Where shame once spoke, let Your kindness speak louder.
Wash my mind with Your Word until my thoughts agree with heaven.
Amen.

Deliverance Declaration

In the name of Jesus Christ, I take every thought captive and make it obey Christ.
I break agreement with fear, shame, and the lie of failure.
I renounce confusion, perfectionism, and self-condemnation.
I receive the mind of Christ—clear, peaceful, and full of faith.
My mistakes are not my identity; they are moments of learning covered by grace.
I am being transformed day by day by the renewing of my mind, and His truth sets me free.

Action Step

Write down one lie you've believed about yourself—especially one tied to failure. Next to it, write a truth from Scripture that cancels that lie.

Example:

Lie: "I'm a failure."
Truth: "I can do all things through Christ who strengthens me."

Keep that truth visible today—on your phone lock screen, mirror, or journal.
Each time you see it, say it out loud until your heart starts to believe it.

Day 16
Forgiving Our Debtors

"Above all else, guard your heart, for everything you do flows from it."
— Proverbs 4:23

"Be kind and compassionate to one another, forgiving each other, just as in Christ God forgave you."
— Ephesians 4:32

**"The Spirit of the Lord is upon Me, because He has anointed Me to heal the brokenhearted,
to proclaim liberty to the captives."**
— Luke 4:18

Teaching

Control and unforgiveness often grow from the same root—**pain**.
When someone hurts you deeply, the heart naturally wants justice.
It wants the other person to see, to admit, to change.
But when that doesn't happen, we start holding the wound close as if our anger could protect us from ever being hurt again.
That's where control sneaks in.

Forgiveness doesn't mean pretending it didn't happen.
It means giving up your *right to punish*.
You stop trying to make them pay, and you let God handle what only He can judge.
You don't forgive because they deserve it—you forgive because you deserve peace.

Unforgiveness is one of fear's quietest control tactics.
It says, *"If I stay angry, I'll stay safe."*

But bitterness doesn't keep pain out—it keeps it *in*.
The heart that refuses to forgive stays locked in the same room as the offense.
You may have built walls to keep others out, but those same walls keep you from healing too.
Forgiveness doesn't mean immediate reconciliation or trust.
You can forgive someone and still keep healthy distance.
Forgiveness is for *you*—it's the release of the weight you were never built to carry.

Entitlement and Unforgiveness: The Trap of Emotional Debt

Entitlement and unforgiveness often walk hand in hand.
When someone wrongs us, it's natural to feel they *owe* us something—an apology, understanding, or at least the acknowledgment of what they did.
But when that "they owe me" mindset takes root, it turns people into **debtors** in our hearts.

That's exactly what Jesus was teaching in the **Lord's Prayer** when He said:

"Forgive us our debts, as we forgive our debtors." (Matthew 6:12)

In other words: *"Father, release me as I release others."*
Every time we hold someone in emotional debt, we also keep ourselves bound to the same offense.
We rehearse the pain, waiting for repayment that may never come.
That debt becomes a form of control—we're silently saying, *"Until you pay me back, I won't let you go."*

But Jesus calls us to live debt-free hearts.
Forgiveness cancels the balance sheet.
It says, *"You don't owe me anymore—because Jesus paid for both of us."*
When we release others from their debt, we release ourselves from

the weight of being their judge.
Freedom always flows both ways.

"Be kind and compassionate… forgiving each other, just as in Christ God forgave you."

God never asks you to give away something He hasn't already given to you.
He forgave you freely, fully, and without holding the debt over your head.
That's the kind of forgiveness that melts bitterness—it flows from love, not willpower.

For many, the hardest part of forgiveness is emotional honesty.
You can't heal what you won't admit hurts.
Letting yourself *feel* the pain isn't weakness—it's the doorway to release.
As you name the hurt, Jesus meets you in it.
He doesn't rush you or shame you; He simply holds the wound until it begins to close.

Forgiveness isn't a single prayer—it's a process.
Some days, you'll have to forgive the same person again.
Each time you do, the grip loosens.
You're teaching your heart to trust God with the outcome instead of trying to control it.

"The Spirit of the Lord is upon Me… to heal the brokenhearted."

Healing happens when love moves where control used to live.
You can't change the past, but you can stop letting it rule your future.

Selah — Pause and Ask:
"Lord, who am I still holding in my heart with resentment or fear?
Have I made anyone my debtor by expecting them to fix what only

You can heal?
Show me how to cancel those debts and live free."

Reflection Questions

1. Who do I still feel anger, resentment, or hurt toward?
2. Have I made anyone my "debtor" by expecting repayment in words or actions?
3. How would it feel to forgive them and trust God to restore what was lost?

(Use the space below to journal your thoughts.)

_____

_____

_____

_____

_____

_____

Prayer for Healing and Release

Father, You see the hurt I've carried and the expectations I've held onto.
I confess that I've made some people debtors in my heart—waiting for apologies, repayment, or understanding.
Today I release those debts.
I forgive my debtors as You have forgiven me.
I give You the right to be my defender and judge.
Heal my heart where bitterness has lived.
Fill that space with peace and compassion.
Amen.

Deliverance Declaration

In the name of Jesus Christ, I break agreement with bitterness, entitlement, and the spirit of unforgiveness.
I release every person I've held in emotional debt, and I cancel their balance in my heart.
I forgive as Christ forgave me—fully and freely.
I release my right to collect repayment, and I trust God to restore what was lost.
I am no longer controlled by pain or offense; I am governed by peace.
The Spirit of the Lord has healed my heart, and I walk in freedom.

Action Step

Write the words *"Paid in Full"* on a small piece of paper.
Think of anyone you've been holding emotionally accountable.
Pray for them by name and say aloud, *"I cancel their debt. They owe me nothing. I am free."*
Keep the paper somewhere visible this week as a reminder that forgiveness cancels emotional debt and opens the door for peace.

Day 17
The Armor of Peace

"And the peace of God, which surpasses all understanding,
will guard your hearts and minds through Christ Jesus."
— Philippians 4:7

"Let the peace of Christ rule in your hearts,
since as members of one body you were called to peace."
— Colossians 3:15

"You will keep in perfect peace those whose minds are stayed on You,
because they trust in You."
— Isaiah 26:3

Teaching

Once you forgive and release what used to control you, something sacred happens—your heart begins to quiet.
That silence may feel strange at first. You've lived for so long in the noise of anxiety, resentment, or overthinking that peace feels almost foreign.
But that stillness you're feeling? It's healing.

The peace of God is not passive—it's *protective*.
Paul says it *guards* your heart and mind. That word *guard* in Greek means *to stand watch like a soldier*.
Peace becomes your armor, not your reward.

Now that you've released pain and control, the enemy will often test those boundaries.
He'll whisper familiar thoughts: *"You're still the same."*
"They don't deserve your forgiveness."

"Nothing's really changed."
That's when you put on your armor—by remembering who you are now.

Peace isn't something you fight *for*; it's something you fight *from*.
When peace rules in your heart, control loses its power.
When peace guards your mind, old fear can knock but can't enter.

"Let the peace of Christ rule in your hearts."

Notice that word: *rule.*
Peace is not a feeling; it's a decision.
It's choosing to stay grounded in love even when you're tempted to return to fear.
It's saying, *"I won't let this situation pull me back into the drama."*

When you sense tension rising, breathe and remember:
Peace isn't fragile—it's fierce.
It's the quiet confidence that God's got this and you don't have to.

You've learned to forgive; now you're learning to stay free.
Peace keeps you from reopening old wounds.
It's how you maintain the healing that forgiveness began.

Selah — Pause and Ask:
"Lord, how can I let Your peace rule when I feel triggered or afraid?
What habits or thoughts are trying to steal what You've restored?"

Reflection Questions

1. What situations most often threaten my peace?
2. How can I respond differently when I feel my calm slipping away?
3. What Scripture can I speak aloud when I feel anxiety or control creeping back in?

(Use the space below to journal your thoughts.)

Prayer for Peace and Protection

Father, thank You for the peace that guards my heart.
I confess that I've often let old thoughts and fears break through that guard.
Today I choose to let Your peace *rule* in me.
Remind me that I don't have to earn calm or chase control—You are my security.
When chaos rises, quiet my spirit.
When fear knocks, let Your Word answer the door.
Teach me to live protected by peace.
Amen.

Deliverance Declaration

In the name of Jesus Christ, I put on the armor of peace.
I renounce fear, anxiety, and emotional reactivity.
I refuse to let worry rule me or to reopen what God has healed.
I declare that the peace of Christ stands guard over my mind and heart.
My emotions are anchored in love, my thoughts aligned with truth, and my spirit rests in God's protection.

Action Step

Every time you feel tension, pause and say aloud:

"Peace, guard my heart."

Take three deep breaths and picture that peace standing like a shield around you.
If someone's words or actions trigger you, silently bless them instead of reacting.
You'll feel the armor hold.
That's God defending what He just restored.

Day 18
Learning to Stay Soft

"I will give you a new heart and put a new spirit within you;
I will remove from you your heart of stone and give you a heart of flesh."
— Ezekiel 36:26

"Blessed are the meek, for they shall inherit the earth."
— Matthew 5:5

"Be completely humble and gentle; be patient, bearing with one another in love."
— Ephesians 4:2

Teaching

After seasons of pain or control, hardness can feel like strength.
You learn to keep your guard up, to never be caught off balance again.
But while hardness may protect you, it also isolates you.
A hard heart can't be hurt—but it also can't be healed.

When God begins restoring peace, He often invites you to do something scarier than forgiving or letting go:
He asks you to stay *soft*.

Soft doesn't mean weak.
Soft means responsive.
It's the heart that can feel conviction without shame, compassion without exhaustion, and love without fear.
It's the heart that trusts God enough to remain open even when people disappoint.

"I will remove your heart of stone and give you a heart of flesh."

The Spirit wants to trade numbness for sensitivity.
Because once your peace returns, the enemy will tempt you to close up again—to stay guarded, cynical, or "unbothered."
But healing isn't about being *unbothered*; it's about being *unbreakable in love.*

When peace meets tenderness, you become strong in a different way.
You can set boundaries without bitterness, correct without cruelty, and walk away without hate.
Your tone softens.
Your reactions slow down.
You start carrying the gentle strength of Jesus—the kind that calmed storms and comforted sinners in the same breath.

Staying soft means letting your compassion outgrow your fear.
It means remembering that people who control or hurt are usually operating from their own emptiness.
You can acknowledge that without excusing it.
Softness doesn't mean saying yes to everything; it means staying kind when you say no.

This is spiritual maturity: to live protected by peace but guided by love.
A tender heart in a cruel world is not a weakness—it's a miracle.

Selah — Pause and Ask:
"Lord, help me stay soft without being naïve.
Teach me the balance between boundaries and compassion, between discernment and tenderness."

Reflection Questions

1. When do I feel tempted to harden my heart or shut down?
2. What does "soft strength" look like in my relationships?

3. How can I stay compassionate without becoming codependent again?

(Use the space below to journal your thoughts.)

Prayer for a Tender Heart

Father, thank You for making my heart new.
I confess that sometimes I confuse protection with hardness.
I don't want to live numb anymore.
Teach me to stay open, teachable, and kind.
Let Your peace guard me and Your love guide me.
When fear tries to close me off, remind me that softness in You is strength.
Amen.

Deliverance Declaration

In the name of Jesus Christ, I renounce hardness, bitterness, and emotional shutdown.
I break agreement with self-protection rooted in fear.
My heart is tender, but it is not weak.
The Spirit of God lives in me, making me gentle, patient, and strong.
I carry peace as armor and love as power.
I will remain soft because God Himself guards my heart.

Action Step

Today, choose one small act of tenderness—
a kind word where you'd normally stay silent,
a gentle tone where you'd usually react.
As you do, whisper: *"Lord, keep my heart soft."*
You'll notice that the more you guard peace,
the easier it becomes to let love flow through you again.

Day 19
Speaking Truth Without Control

"**The fear of man brings a snare,
but whoever trusts in the Lord shall be safe.**"
— Proverbs 29:25

"**Let your 'Yes' be 'Yes,' and your 'No,' be 'No.'**"
— Matthew 5:37

"**Speak the truth in love, growing in every way more and more like Christ.**"
— Ephesians 4:15

"**For God has not given us a spirit of fear, but of power and of love and of a sound mind.**"
— 2 Timothy 1:7

Teaching

When you begin to heal, God restores something powerful—your voice.
Not the loud one that argues, or the quiet one that hides, but the *true* voice that speaks with peace and conviction.

Many of us learned to survive by saying what people wanted to hear or by avoiding truth to keep the peace.
That's not humility—it's fear.
The fear of man keeps you trapped in patterns of silence, compromise, and people-pleasing.
It convinces you that keeping others happy is safer than obeying God.
But Scripture says the fear of man is a *snare*—a trap that keeps you from walking in freedom.

When you fear people's opinions, you lose your ability to discern God's instructions.
You'll hesitate when He says "speak," and rush when He says "wait."
You can't fully obey the Lord while monitoring everyone's reactions.
Obedience and approval don't mix.

Boundaries are not rebellion—they are obedience.
When you say *no* because the Holy Spirit leads you to, you are honoring God more than man.
When you say *yes* from conviction instead of pressure, you release peace instead of resentment.
Boundaries define your obedience line—they protect what God has healed.

"The fear of man brings a snare, but whoever trusts in the Lord is safe."

Safety doesn't come from being liked; it comes from being led.
Trusting God frees you to speak the truth in love without manipulation or apology.
That's where courage begins—when you care more about God's voice than anyone else's reaction.

Jesus modeled this perfectly.
He loved deeply but didn't bend to people's expectations.
He set boundaries without bitterness and truth without tone-policing.
That's what your healing is preparing you for—to speak with *holy clarity* instead of human fear.

Selah — Pause and Ask:
"Lord, where has the fear of man kept me quiet when You wanted me to speak?
Show me where pleasing people has led to disobedience."

Reflection Questions

1. Where have I avoided truth to keep peace or approval?
2. What would trusting God more than people look like in my communication?
3. Which boundary is the Holy Spirit asking me to set that I've been afraid to because of others' reactions?

(Use the space below to journal your thoughts.)

Prayer for Courage and Clarity

Father, thank You for giving me a voice.
I confess that I've let fear of people's opinions silence my obedience.
I've confused being nice with being faithful.
Forgive me for valuing acceptance over Your approval.
Teach me to speak the truth in love, to set boundaries without guilt, and to follow Your peace even when others misunderstand.
I trust You to protect me as I obey.
Amen.

Deliverance Declaration

In the name of Jesus Christ, I renounce the fear of man and every spirit of people-pleasing.
I break agreement with silence born of shame and speech driven by control.
I receive a Spirit of power, love, and a sound mind.
My words are anchored in truth and covered in peace.
I will obey God even when it costs me approval.
The Lord is my safety; His peace is my guard.

Action Step

Think of one area where you've stayed silent out of fear.
Write what obedience would look like instead—what truth you'd speak or what boundary you'd set if you trusted God fully.
Pray Proverbs 29:25 aloud and declare:

"Lord, You are my safety. I will trust You, not the opinions of man."

Day 20
The Right Kind of Thirst

"Jesus said to her, 'Give Me a drink.' ...
'Whoever drinks of the water that I shall give him will never thirst.
But the water that I shall give him will become in him a fountain of water springing up into everlasting life.'"
— John 4 : 7 , 14

"To the thirsty I will give water without cost from the spring of the water of life."
— Revelation 21 : 6

"Blessed are those who hunger and thirst for righteousness, for they will be filled."
— Matthew 5 : 6

Teaching

When Jesus met the Samaritan woman at the well, He didn't start with correction — He started with a *request*.

"Give Me a drink."

Before He offered her living water, He invited her to *worship*.
He knew that if she poured out first — if she turned her attention and affection toward Him — He could fill her with something that would never run dry.

That's the secret of this story: **the thirsty get Jesus.**
She came to draw natural water, but He came to satisfy a spiritual thirst she didn't even recognize.

Five broken relationships later, she was still looking for love that could only be found in Him.

When your soul is thirsty, it will drink from whatever is closest — people, performance, attention, even ministry.
Control often begins right here: we grasp for others to fill what only worship was meant to satisfy.

But Jesus meets us at our wells — the places we've gone back to again and again — and says,

"If you knew the gift of God and who it is who asks you for a drink…"

He doesn't shame our thirst; He sanctifies it.
He teaches us that thirst isn't weakness — it's *invitation*.
The woman's honesty about her emptiness became the very doorway to revelation:

"Sir, give me this water."

When you worship Him first — when you give Him drink — He fills you in return.
Worship quenches the soul so you stop trying to drink from people. Only full hearts can love without control.

Steffany Gretzinger calls this "remaining thirsty"—never so self-sufficient that you forget your need for Him.
The bride that forgets her thirst becomes proud; the bride that stays thirsty becomes radiant.

So before you pour out for anyone else, pause and drink deeply.
He's not just the *Water*; He's the *Well*.

Selah — Pause and Ask:
"Lord, what wells have I been drawing from instead of You?
Teach me to worship before I pour."

Reflection Questions

1. What do I reach for when I feel empty or unseen?
2. How can I turn my longing into worship instead of control?
3. What would it look like to stay thirsty for Him each day?

(Use the space below to journal your thoughts.)

_____
_____
_____
_____
_____
_____

Prayer of Worship and Filling

Jesus, You are the Living Water.
Forgive me for trying to satisfy my soul with people or performance.
Today I give You drink through my worship.
Fill the empty places with Your presence.
Teach me to stay thirsty for You, not dependent on others.
Let Your Spirit become a fountain within me that never runs dry.
Amen.

Deliverance Declaration

In the name of Jesus Christ, I renounce false comfort and soulish attachments.
I break agreement with idolatry that looks like need.
My thirst belongs to God alone.
I will drink freely from the Living Water and overflow with love that does not control.
I am filled, satisfied, and free.

Action Step

Find a quiet moment today to worship without asking for anything.
Play a song that fixes your eyes on Jesus and simply pour out love to Him.
Then sit in stillness and let Him fill you.
Notice how the need for people's approval or attention begins to fade.
That's what happens when you drink from the Well instead of the world.

Day 21
Letting Go of the Door

"I am the door. If anyone enters by Me, he will be saved."
— John 10:9

"Not by might, nor by power, but by My Spirit," says the Lord of hosts.
— Zechariah 4:6

"No one can come to Me unless the Father who sent Me draws them."
— John 6:44

Teaching

Sometimes control looks spiritual.
You pray, fast, and stand in faith for someone you love,
but slowly your intercession turns into *interference.*
Without realizing it, you're holding the door open for them,
waiting and watching, hoping they'll walk through —
and exhausting yourself in the process.

Earlier this year, worship leader **Steffany Gretzinger** shared a vision that captures this perfectly.
She saw a wooden doorstop—wedged beneath a door—and the Lord told her, *"That's you."*
She had been trying to hold the door open for people she loved.
It felt noble, even holy.
But then Jesus said, *"I'm the Door. That's not your job."*

When you hold the door open for someone, you're not fully entering yourself.
You stay half in, half out—trying to monitor their progress.
It looks like love, but it's really *fear wearing a ministry badge.*

It's the belief that your effort can make someone else surrender faster.

The truth is humbling:
You cannot save, convict, or transform another heart.
Only the Holy Spirit can.
And when you try to do His work, even with good intentions, you end up stuck in the threshold—burned out, disappointed, and spiritually divided.

Letting go of the door means trusting God with their journey.
It means you walk all the way through obedience while leaving the door unlocked, not forced open.
Your job is to love, pray, and *model* freedom—not to manufacture it for others.

That's not indifference; that's faith.
When you release control, you make room for the Holy Spirit to move in ways your striving never could.

"Only the Holy Spirit draws hearts."

So stop being the doorstop.
Be the *bride* who walks through the Door, radiant with His love.
Because when you truly go in, His presence on you begins to "drip" on others—and that's what will draw them through.

Selah — Pause and Ask:
"Lord, am I trying to hold the door open for someone You've asked me to release?
Teach me to trust Your timing and stop standing in the doorway."

Reflection Questions

1. Who am I trying to fix, save, or push closer to God right now?

2. How does it make me feel when they don't respond the way I hope?
3. What would letting go look like in this relationship?

(Use the space below to journal your thoughts.)

Prayer of Release

Father, forgive me for trying to play the part of the Holy Spirit.
I've stood in the doorway, holding it open for others,
believing that if I prayed harder or waited longer, they'd come through.
I release every person I've tried to rescue.
You are the Door; You are the Savior.
I trust Your timing, Your conviction, and Your love.
Teach me to walk all the way through—to live fully in freedom,
and let my life be the invitation that draws others to You.
Amen.

Deliverance Declaration

In the name of Jesus Christ, I break agreement with false responsibility, control, and spiritual exhaustion.
I am not the doorstop; I am a child of God, free to walk through the Door.

I release every person I've tried to save, fix, or monitor.
I trust the Holy Spirit to do what only He can do.
I live fully in God's presence and rest in His perfect love.

Action Step

Take a moment to visualize that person or situation you've been "holding the door" for.
Now, in your mind, let go of the handle.
See Jesus standing there instead.
Say aloud: *"Lord, You are the Door. I trust You with them."*
Then turn and walk all the way through—into peace, freedom, and rest.

Day 22
Love Without Strings Attached

"Love never fails."
— 1 Corinthians 13:8

"Do everything in love."
— 1 Corinthians 16:14

"And whatever you do, do it heartily, as to the Lord and not to men."
— Colossians 3:23

Teaching

One of the hardest lessons in freedom is learning to love without needing anything back.
When you've spent years giving to get—approval, affection, peace, validation—real love can feel risky.
You wonder, *"What if they don't appreciate it? What if they take advantage of me again?"*

That's the voice of old fear trying to measure love by results.
But love, in its purest form, isn't transactional—it's transformational.
It's not about *what happens after you give*; it's about *who you become when you do.*

"Do everything in love."

God's love doesn't calculate outcomes; it simply obeys.
Jesus loved Judas, even knowing the betrayal was coming.
He washed his feet anyway.

That's what perfect love looks like—power under control, kindness without demand, mercy without manipulation.

We see another powerful picture of this in **1 Samuel 24**.
David was hiding in a cave while King Saul hunted him to kill him. When Saul entered the same cave, unguarded, David's men urged him to strike—"This is your chance!"
But David only cut off a corner of Saul's robe, refusing to harm him. Later he said, *"I will not stretch out my hand against my lord, for he is the Lord's anointed."*

That was **mercy without manipulation**.
David didn't spare Saul to make him feel guilty or to secure his favor.
He acted from honor, not outcome.
He chose obedience over opportunity.
Mercy like that comes from hearts no longer trying to control the story—hearts that trust God to vindicate, promote, and heal.

When you're healed, you no longer love to manage outcomes—you love because love has managed *you*.
You stop performing for acceptance and start giving from abundance.
This is what freedom feels like: to love, release, and rest, trusting that God is responsible for what happens next.

This doesn't mean staying in unhealthy situations or excusing harm. Boundaries and love coexist.
But the difference is motivation—you no longer draw lines to punish; you draw them to protect peace.
You love fully *and* wisely, giving without control and walking away without resentment.

"Whatever you do, do it heartily, as to the Lord and not to men."

When you love as unto the Lord, you can't lose.
Even when people don't respond the way you hope, heaven records the obedience.

Your worth isn't tied to how someone receives you; it's anchored in how God loves you because we are rooted and grounded in love.

This is maturity—when you love without needing to be seen, thanked, or validated.
When love is your lifestyle, not your leverage.

Selah — Pause and Ask:
"Lord, show me where I've attached strings to love.
Teach me to love like David—merciful, but not manipulative."

Reflection Questions

1. Where have I been loving others with hidden expectations or conditions?
2. What fear rises in me when love isn't returned the way I hope?
3. How can I show mercy like David—choosing obedience over outcome?

(Use the space below to journal your thoughts.)

_____
_____
_____
_____
_____
_____

Prayer for Unconditional Love

Father, thank You for loving me without conditions.
Forgive me for the times I've shown kindness expecting change in return.
Teach me to love like You—freely, joyfully, without demand.
When I give, let it be from fullness, not need.
When I show mercy, let it be pure, not manipulative.

Help me choose obedience over outcome and leave results in Your hands.
Amen.

Deliverance Declaration

In the name of Jesus Christ, I break agreement with fear, manipulation, and conditional love.
I renounce false responsibility and the need for recognition.
Like David, I will show mercy without control, honor without fear, and love without strings.
I am a vessel of divine love—full, free, and fearless.
Love never fails because it flows from the heart of God.

Action Step

Think of a situation where you could show mercy but have hesitated because you feared being misunderstood.
Ask God for the strength to respond in love—not to prove a point, but to honor Him.
Say aloud:

"Lord, I release the outcome. I choose mercy without manipulation."

That's the sound of freedom—loving with no strings, just grace.

Day 23
Trusting God with Your Growth

**"Being confident of this very thing,
that He who has begun a good work in you
will complete it until the day of Jesus Christ."**
— *Philippians 1:6*

**"We all, with unveiled face,
beholding as in a mirror the glory of the Lord,
are being transformed into the same image from glory to glory."**
— *2 Corinthians 3:18*

**"The path of the righteous is like the light of dawn,
which shines brighter and brighter until full day."**
— *Proverbs 4:18*

Teaching

Freedom isn't a finish line—it's a *lifelong unfolding.*
You're not meant to *arrive*; you're meant to *become.*

Healing happens layer by layer, season by season.
There will be moments of sudden breakthrough and moments of slow, hidden growth.
Both are holy.

But when you've lived in control, process feels uncomfortable.
You'll want to measure progress—to grade your growth and know how you're doing.
That's the old mindset creeping back, trying to turn transformation into performance.

The apostle Paul reminds us,

"He who began a good work in you will carry it to completion."

God is not grading you—He's growing you.
Yet many of us become our own teachers and judges.
We read the Word, gain knowledge, and then start *testing* ourselves with it instead of letting it transform us.

Dan Mohler once warned about this trap:

You can be sincere but live under constant self-judgment. You read your Bible, but instead of letting grace make you what you're reading, you compare yourself to it and start grading your own test. The Word that was meant to inspire you ends up condemning you—not because God is judging you, but because you're judging yourself. You become the teacher and the student, taking the test and scoring it, deciding how valuable you are based on performance. But you're not the teacher—you're the beloved student. You wake up and enjoy being His.

That's what happens when we let *knowledge replace intimacy*.
If you read Scripture without relating to the Author, the letter of the Word can turn on you.
It will highlight where you fall short instead of showing you where you're called to grow.
The enemy loves to twist conviction into condemnation, making you believe you're failing when you're actually learning.

God never invited you to take your own test.
He invited you to trust the process—to stay close enough for His grace to keep shaping you.
Your role isn't to measure your progress; it's to remain in relationship.

Growth isn't about *trying harder*—it's about *staying closer*.
When you keep walking with Him, even in weakness, you'll notice small changes that prove His Spirit is working.
Patience replaces panic.
Peace replaces pressure.
Love replaces self-judgment.

"We are being transformed from glory to glory."

Each stage reveals more of Him and less of fear.
You are not behind; you are becoming.

Selah — Pause and Ask:
"Lord, where have I been grading myself instead of trusting You to grow me?
Teach me to enjoy becoming instead of condemning myself for not being finished."

Reflection Questions

1. Where do I tend to judge myself most harshly?
2. How can I shift from measuring progress to enjoying relationship?
3. What fruit of growth has quietly appeared in me this season?

(Use the space below to journal your thoughts.)

Prayer for Trusting the Process

Father, thank You that You're not in a hurry with me.
You're patient, kind, and faithful.
Forgive me for grading myself, comparing my growth, or believing

I'm behind.
I don't want to take my own test anymore.
I want to rest in Your classroom of grace, where love is the lesson and transformation is the outcome.
Teach me to see myself through Your eyes—
in progress, on purpose, and deeply loved.
Amen.

Deliverance Declaration

In the name of Jesus Christ, I renounce self-judgment, comparison, and perfectionism.
I break agreement with condemnation and striving.
I am not the teacher and the student; I am the beloved being transformed by grace.
I refuse to grade myself by human standards.
The Word inspires me; it no longer accuses me.
I am becoming who God created me to be—faithfully, freely, and fully His.

Action Step

Each time you're tempted to analyze how "well" you're doing, stop and say aloud:

"Lord, I trust You with my growth. I'm not my own judge—I'm Your student."

Then spend a few quiet minutes simply enjoying His presence.
Let His love teach you what no score ever could.

Day 24
The Rest of Faith

"Come to Me, all you who labor and are heavy laden, and I will give you rest."
— Matthew 11:28

"In returning and rest you shall be saved; in quietness and trust shall be your strength."
— Isaiah 30:15

"For we who have believed do enter that rest."
— Hebrews 4:3

"Be still, and know that I am God."
— Psalm 46:10

Teaching

Once you stop grading yourself, the next battle is the pressure to *keep performing spiritually.*
Even in healing, control can disguise itself as "spiritual diligence."
You start thinking, *Am I growing fast enough? Am I doing enough?*

But true transformation isn't powered by pressure — it's sustained by **peace.**
Jesus never invited you to *work harder*; He invited you to *rest deeper.*

This is what Hebrews 4 calls **the rest of faith**:

"For we who have believed do enter that rest."

Faith's highest expression isn't striving — it's *trusting.*
It's when you stop trying to prove you believe and start living as

though God is faithful.
Rest is not laziness; it's confidence that His grace is doing what your effort never could.

When you rest in His presence, you return to the posture you were designed for — dependence.
You stop laboring to become and start abiding as beloved.
Rest is what faith looks like when it's mature.

"Let us be diligent to enter that rest."

That sounds paradoxical — work hard to rest — but it means protecting that peace like treasure.
You fight every thought that says, *"I should be doing more."*
You silence every fear that whispers, *"I'm falling behind."*
Because when you rest in faith, you're standing on the finished work of Jesus.

We see this perfectly in the story of **Mary and Martha** (Luke 10:38-42).
Martha was busy serving — anxious, distracted, and overwhelmed — trying to please Jesus with her effort.
Mary simply sat at His feet and listened.
Jesus gently said,

"Martha, Martha, you are worried and upset about many things, but only one thing is needed. Mary has chosen the better part."

That's the rest of faith.
Mary wasn't being lazy; she was receiving.
She chose intimacy over activity — relationship over results.
Her stillness was worship, and her faith gave her access to what Martha's striving never could.

Pressure says, *"Earn it."*
Faith says, *"It's finished."*
Rest is not found in doing nothing — it's found in trusting completely.

Selah — Pause and Ask:
"Lord, where have I confused activity with intimacy?
Teach me to live from the rest of faith — confident in Your finished work."

Reflection Questions

1. In what areas of my life do I still feel pressured to perform spiritually?
2. How can I protect my peace and remain in the rest of faith?
3. What would "sitting at His feet" look like in my daily routine?

(Use the space below to journal your thoughts.)

Prayer for Rest

Father, thank You for the invitation to rest.
Forgive me for striving to earn what You've already given.
I lay down anxiety, performance, and self-reliance.
Teach me to trust like Mary — to sit at Your feet and receive.
Help me enter the rest of faith, where my soul can breathe again.
In quietness and confidence, make me strong.
Amen.

Deliverance Declaration

In the name of Jesus Christ, I renounce striving, burnout, and the fear of falling behind.
I break agreement with pressure and perfectionism.
I receive the rest of faith — complete trust in the finished work of Christ.
His peace rules my heart; His presence is my dwelling place.
I rest, I trust, and I grow in grace.

Action Step

Find a quiet moment today and simply sit at His feet.
No requests, no lists — just worship.
Whisper:

"I believe, therefore I rest."

Let peace replace pressure.
As you rest in faith, you'll notice something beautiful: growth happening without striving — love deepening without fear.
That's the fruit of peace.

Day 25
Becoming the River

"Whoever believes in Me, as the Scripture has said, out of his heart will flow rivers of living water."
— *John 7:38*

"The generous soul will be made rich, and he who waters will himself be watered."
— *Proverbs 11:25*

"My cup overflows."
— *Psalm 23:5*

Teaching

There comes a moment in healing when you realize you're no longer living thirsty.
You're not begging for love, attention, or validation anymore — you're *overflowing* with what once felt missing.
That's the fruit of abiding.

Jesus never designed His followers to survive on occasional sips of His presence;
He called us to become fountains — *"rivers of living water."*
When your life flows from His fullness, you stop chasing what you already have.
Love stops being something you look for and becomes something you *carry*.

Remember the Samaritan woman?
Once she drank the Living Water, she dropped her jar and ran to tell others.
She didn't need to draw from the old well anymore because she *became* one.

Her encounter with Jesus transformed her from a seeker into a source.

That's what grace does — it fills until it spills.
You can't give what you don't have, but when you're filled, giving becomes effortless.
You forgive without forcing it, serve without resentment, and love without losing yourself.

"The generous soul will be made rich."

Notice the flow: you pour out, and God refills.
That's not depletion — that's divine circulation.
You become a conduit, not a container.
When your motive is love, not obligation, you'll find His Spirit constantly replenishing you.

Overflow doesn't mean perfection or constant emotional high;
it means being so secure in His love that you no longer panic when others can't give it back.
It's freedom from spiritual codependency — because your Source never runs dry.

This is the *rest of faith in motion.*
You're not trying to earn, impress, or control; you're living as one who has received.
That's why peace follows you — because it's flowing *through* you.

Selah — Pause and Ask:
"Lord, where am I still living like a seeker instead of a source?
Fill me again until Your love overflows into every part of my life."

Biblical Example — The Feeding of the 5,000

When the disciples saw thousands of hungry people, they panicked: *"We don't have enough."*
But Jesus took what they had — five loaves and two fish — lifted it

to heaven, and gave thanks.
Then He *broke it and blessed it.*
As they distributed what seemed too little, it multiplied in their hands.

That's what overflow looks like: **thankfulness turns lack into abundance.**
You don't wait to feel full before giving — you trust that as you pour, He fills.
The more they gave, the more there was to give.

God never asked you to produce the miracle — just to keep passing out what He gives you.

Reflection Questions

1. What areas of my life still operate from "not enough"?
2. Where do I feel God calling me to pour out what I already have?
3. How can I practice gratitude and generosity this week as acts of overflow?

(Use the space below to journal your thoughts.)

_____
_____
_____
_____
_____

Prayer for Overflow

Jesus, thank You for filling every empty place in me.
I don't want to live as a seeker anymore; I want to live as a source.
Teach me to trust Your abundance, not my ability.
As I pour out love, joy, and grace, keep my heart connected to You.

Let rivers of living water flow from me — refreshing everyone around me.
Amen.

Deliverance Declaration

In the name of Jesus Christ, I renounce the spirit of lack and spiritual poverty.
I break agreement with fear of depletion and striving for approval.
I receive the abundance of Christ.
My cup overflows; my life is a river of His love.
I live from fullness, not emptiness.
I am not a seeker of validation; I am a vessel of overflow.

Action Step

Find one small way to pour out today —
encourage someone, give generously, pray for a stranger, or speak peace over someone's storm.
As you do, whisper:

"I give from overflow, not obligation."

You'll sense His joy replenishing you even as you pour —

Day 26
Gratitude In The Midst of Pain

"Enter His gates with thanksgiving
and His courts with praise;
give thanks to Him and bless His name."
— *Psalm 100:4*

"In everything give thanks, for this is the will of God in Christ Jesus for you."
— *1 Thessalonians 5:18*

"Rejoice in the Lord always; again I will say, rejoice."
— *Philippians 4:4*

"I am more than the bad things that happen to me."
— *Nightbirde (Jane Marczewski)*

Teaching

Gratitude isn't denial of pain — it's faith in the middle of it.
It's how we *enter* God's presence, shift our perspective, and open our hearts again.
When you give thanks, you step through the gates of His presence, leaving behind the noise of fear and stepping into the atmosphere of heaven.

"Enter His gates with thanksgiving."

Thanksgiving is the key that unlocks His peace.
It reminds your soul that no matter what's been lost, *He's still here.*

Singer and songwriter **Nightbirde (Jane Marczewski)** lived this truth in one of the most beautiful and heartbreaking ways.

Diagnosed with terminal cancer, she stood on the stage of *America's Got Talent* with a radiant smile and a trembling voice that carried the fragrance of heaven.
When the judges asked how she could stay so joyful, she simply said,

"You can't wait until life isn't hard anymore before you decide to be happy."

Her gratitude wasn't rooted in circumstance — it was rooted in *relationship*.
She had found something in God that cancer couldn't touch.
In her writings, she said,

"I am more than the bad things that happen to me."

That's the essence of gratitude: choosing to believe that what happened *to you* is not stronger than what God is doing *in you*.
Gratitude doesn't erase pain; it redeems it.
It turns suffering into song, wounds into worship, and sorrow into seed.

Nightbirde's life preached this message without words:
Thankfulness is how the broken stay beautiful.
It's how faith survives the fire and comes out glowing.
Even in dying, she showed the world what it means to truly live —
full of grace, full of light, full of gratitude.

Gratitude doesn't just say "it's okay."
It says, "He's still good."

Biblical Example — The One Leper Who Returned

Ten lepers were healed by Jesus, but only one came back to give thanks (Luke 17:11–19).
The others received healing, but the thankful one received *wholeness*.
Jesus said to him,

"Rise and go; your faith has made you whole."

Gratitude finished what healing started.
It kept the man connected to the Healer, not just the healing.
Just like Nightbirde, he didn't let his past pain silence his praise.
He used thanksgiving as a doorway into a deeper kind of freedom.

When you live thankful, you live aware —
aware of grace, aware of progress, aware of presence.
You stop saying, *"I'll be grateful when…"*
and start saying,
"I'm grateful now, because God is with me."

That's the heart of true worship — gratitude that refuses to wait for perfect conditions before giving praise.

Selah — Pause and Ask:
"Lord, what have I overlooked that deserves my thanks today?
Teach me to see my story through Your goodness, not my grief."

Reflection Questions

1. What painful chapter of my life could become a testimony if I thanked God through it?
2. How can I practice gratitude today, not because life is easy, but because He is faithful?
3. What am I thankful for right now that I once prayed for in tears?

(Use the space below to journal your thoughts.)

Prayer of Thanksgiving

Father, thank You that I am more than the bad things that happen to me.
Thank You for turning ashes into beauty and pain into praise.
Teach me to live like Nightbirde — to sing in the storm,
to find You in the waiting, and to choose gratitude even when life is hard.
I enter Your gates with thanksgiving today,
not because everything is perfect, but because You are.
Amen.

Deliverance Declaration

In the name of Jesus Christ, I renounce bitterness, self-pity, and despair.
I break agreement with the lie that my pain defines me.
I declare that I am more than the bad things that happen to me.
I choose gratitude over grief, worship over worry, and faith over fear.
My heart is full of thanksgiving and my life is a song of praise.

Action Step

Think of a situation that has caused you deep pain or disappointment.
Write it down, and underneath it, list one way God has revealed Himself in that place.
Then say aloud,

"Thank You, Lord. I am more than what I've been through."

That moment of gratitude becomes your worship.
That worship becomes your strength.
And that strength becomes your overflow.

Day 27
Joy Through Pain

"Looking unto Jesus, the author and finisher of our faith, who for the joy that was set before Him endured the cross, despising the shame, and has sat down at the right hand of the throne of God."
— *Hebrews 12:2*

"The joy of the Lord is your strength."
— *Nehemiah 8:10*

"Father, forgive them, for they do not know what they are doing."
— *Luke 23:34*

Teaching

Joy is not the absence of pain — it's the presence of purpose.
Real joy doesn't come from what's happening *around* you, but from what's alive *within* you.

When Jesus faced the cross, He didn't endure because it felt good.
He endured because of the *joy set before Him* — the joy of reconciliation, of redemption, of seeing you free and whole.
That joy gave Him strength to stay where love required Him to stand.
He wasn't held there by nails, but by love.

"Father, forgive them, for they do not know what they are doing."

Even as He hung on the cross, Jesus released His adversaries.
He didn't see them as enemies to resent, but as blind hearts in need

of mercy.
That's the secret of joy — when love becomes stronger than offense.

As Dan Mohler often teaches,

"The only reason a spouse or anyone may try to abuse you is because they don't see the value of their own life. We get hurt by them instead of hurting for them."

That's what Jesus modeled perfectly on the cross.
He didn't get hurt *by* His accusers — He hurt *for* them.
He understood that they didn't see who they truly were.
Their blindness didn't change His love; His love became the remedy for their blindness.

That's the kind of joy that overcomes evil — the joy that comes from seeing beyond someone's behavior into their brokenness.
It's compassion born from identity.

When you know who you are in Christ, you don't absorb other people's wounds — you intercede for their healing.
You don't internalize their rejection — you respond with redemption.
That's supernatural joy: to look at pain through love's eyes and still say, *"Father, forgive them."*

"The joy of the Lord is your strength."

Joy is what allows you to forgive without bitterness, to endure without collapsing, to love when others hate.
It's not pretending the hurt didn't happen; it's refusing to let the hurt define you.
You are not what was done to you — you are what He's done *for* you.

When you live from that truth, offense loses its power, and compassion becomes your new reflex.
You stop getting hurt *by* people and start hurting *for* them — the same way Jesus did.

Selah — Pause and Ask:
"Lord, teach me to see people the way You do — not as threats or enemies,
but as hearts who need to know who they are.
Let Your joy make me strong enough to love them."

Reflection Questions

1. Who has wounded me deeply, and how might their actions come from not knowing their own value?
2. How can I respond with compassion instead of resentment?
3. What joy has God set before me that helps me endure hardship with faith?

(Use the space below to journal your thoughts.)

Prayer for Enduring Joy

Jesus, thank You for showing me what love under pressure looks like.
You endured the cross because You saw joy beyond the pain.
Teach me to live like that — to see purpose in my trials and people through Your compassion.
When I'm hurt, help me remember that others often act from their own brokenness.

Let me respond not with bitterness but with mercy.
Fill me with Your joy — the joy that forgives, the joy that endures, the joy that heals everything it touches.
Amen.

Deliverance Declaration

In the name of Jesus Christ, I renounce offense, resentment, and self-pity.
I break agreement with the lie that I am what others have done to me.
I forgive those who have hurt me, and I bless them to know their true worth.
I receive the joy of the Lord as my strength.
I am not hurt by them; I hurt for them.
I live in the same joy that carried Jesus through the cross.

Action Step

Think of someone whose actions have deeply wounded you.
Today, instead of replaying the pain, whisper:

"Father, forgive them — they don't know who they are."

Then thank God that you *do* know who you are — His beloved child.
That realization will release a river of peace in you.
That's the moment when joy becomes your strength —
when you love like Jesus, even through the cross.

Day 28
Stewarding the Oil in Our Life

"The Spirit of the Lord God is upon Me,
because the Lord has anointed Me
to preach good news to the poor;
He has sent Me to heal the brokenhearted…
to give them beauty for ashes,
the oil of joy for mourning,
the garment of praise for the spirit of heaviness."
— *Isaiah 61:1–3*

"Weeping may endure for a night,
but joy comes in the morning."
— *Psalm 30:5*

"At midnight the cry rang out: 'Here's the bridegroom! Come out to meet him!'
Then all the virgins woke up and trimmed their lamps.
The foolish ones said to the wise, 'Give us some of your oil; our lamps are going out.'
'No,' they replied, 'there may not be enough for both us and you. Instead, go to those who sell oil and buy some for yourselves.'"
— *Matthew 25:6–9*

Teaching

There comes a moment in every healing journey when the Holy Spirit begins to trade your sorrow for strength.
You no longer just survive the storm — you begin to dance in the rain.
That's the miracle of grace: God doesn't just take your pain away; He transforms it into something sacred.

"To give them the oil of joy for mourning."

Oil represents anointing — the empowerment of the Holy Spirit that heals what was broken and redeems what was wasted.
You don't just receive comfort; you receive *power to comfort others.*
But that power must stay connected to its Source.

Sometimes, in our compassion, we try to pour our oil into others — to comfort, fix, or rescue them — and it feels noble.
But if we're not careful, we begin to step into a role that only the Holy Spirit was meant to fill.

That's what Jesus illustrated in the **parable of the ten virgins.**
For years, many of us read that story and thought the wise virgins seemed selfish — why wouldn't they share?
But this wasn't about generosity; it was about *stewardship.*
They couldn't give away what only intimacy could produce.
Oil represents personal relationship — you can't borrow someone else's connection to God.

There comes a time when the most loving thing you can do is step back and let the Holy Spirit do His job.
If you keep trying to be someone's constant comforter, rescuer, or prophet, you can unknowingly become their *source.*
And the moment you become their source, control sneaks in — because they start depending on you instead of God.

Healthy love says,

"I will pray for you, but I cannot pour for you."

Your oil is sacred. It's cultivated in worship, obedience, and surrender.
It's not selfish to protect it — it's wise.
You can't light another person's lamp by emptying your own.
Instead, you shine as a reminder that oil is available to anyone willing to seek the Giver.

This is how the *oil of joy* keeps flowing — not by giving it all away, but by staying full and letting the overflow anoint others.

Selah — Pause and Ask:
"Lord, have I tried to be someone's source instead of pointing them to You?
Teach me to love without controlling, and to help without replacing Your Spirit."

Reflection Questions

1. Have I been trying to fix or rescue someone instead of letting the Holy Spirit work in them?
2. How can I stay full of oil while still being compassionate toward others?
3. What boundaries help me give from overflow, not depletion?

(Use the space below to journal your thoughts.)

Prayer for the Oil of Joy and Discernment

Holy Spirit, thank You for being the true Comforter.
Forgive me for the times I've tried to carry burdens You never asked me to.
Teach me to stay filled with Your oil and to trust You to work in others' lives.
Help me love without controlling and support without rescuing.
Pour fresh oil on my heart — the oil of joy that lifts heaviness,

and the wisdom that protects intimacy.
Amen.

Deliverance Declaration

In the name of Jesus Christ, I break agreement with false responsibility and emotional control.
I renounce the lie that I must be everyone's comforter.
I am not the source — the Holy Spirit is.
I receive the oil of joy for my own heart, and I trust Him to pour into others.
My lamp will not run dry, and my boundaries will stay blessed.

Action Step

If you've been over-caring or over-carrying someone, release them to God today.
Say aloud:

"Holy Spirit, I give them back to You. Be their comforter and guide."

Then spend time refilling your own lamp — worship, pray, and receive fresh oil.
When your lamp is full, your love shines brighter — not from exhaustion, but from overflow.

Day 29
Beauty for Ashes

"He gives beauty for ashes,
the oil of joy for mourning,
the garment of praise for the spirit of heaviness;
that they might be called trees of righteousness,
the planting of the Lord,
that He may be glorified."
— *Isaiah 61:3*

"And we know that all things work together for good
to those who love God,
to those who are the called according to His purpose."
— *Romans 8:28*

"What you meant for evil, God meant for good."
— *Genesis 50:20*

Teaching

Ashes are what remain after something has burned — they represent loss, endings, and the things you thought would never rise again.
But God sees ashes differently.
Where you see destruction, He sees potential for beauty.
Where you see an ending, He sees a *beginning in disguise.*

"He gives beauty for ashes."

That word *"for"* means *"in exchange for."*
It's a divine trade.
You bring Him the remnants — the mistakes, the heartbreaks, the losses — and He gives you something only heaven can make: beauty born from redemption.

This is not about pretending the fire never happened.
It's about realizing the fire didn't destroy you — it refined you.
You're not the same person who went into it.
Your compassion is deeper, your vision is clearer, your love is purer.
That's beauty.

Joseph understood this after years of betrayal, false accusation, and imprisonment.
When he finally stood before the very brothers who had sold him, he said,

"You meant it for evil, but God meant it for good."

That's the moment ashes turned to beauty — not when Joseph reached the palace, but when he saw *purpose in the pain.*
When you can look at what tried to destroy you and see God's fingerprints in it, you've entered redemption's territory.

"All things work together for good…"

Notice it doesn't say *all things are good,* but *all things work together* for it.
Even the ashes.
Especially the ashes.

Sometimes the hardest part of healing is allowing God to reinterpret your story.
You've spent years labeling chapters as "failure" or "waste," but heaven reads them as "training" and "trust."
The moments that broke you were also the moments that built something unshakeable in you — faith that no storm can take.

Beauty isn't perfection; it's perspective.
It's when your scars start shining because they tell a story of grace.

Selah — Pause and Ask:
"Lord, show me the beauty You see in the ashes I still carry.
Give me heaven's eyes for my own story."

Reflection Questions

1. What part of my story have I struggled to see any good in?
2. How has God already begun redeeming that pain?
3. What does it mean for me to wear a "garment of praise" instead of heaviness?

(Use the space below to journal your thoughts.)

Prayer for Seeing Beauty

Father, thank You for seeing beauty where I saw only brokenness.
Help me to trust that no season of my life was wasted.
I give You my ashes — every regret, every disappointment, every loss.
Teach me to see my story through Your eyes.
Wrap me in Your garment of praise until I recognize myself again — not as the one who burned, but as the one You rebuilt.
Amen.

Deliverance Declaration

In the name of Jesus Christ, I break agreement with shame, regret, and self-blame.
I renounce the lie that my past disqualifies me.
I receive the beauty of redemption in place of the ashes of my pain.
I am the planting of the Lord, strong and radiant.
My story glorifies Him — every chapter, every scar, every resurrection.

Action Step

Find a quiet moment today to revisit one memory that still carries pain.
Instead of asking "why," ask "what now, Lord?"
Then write one sentence of *gratitude* about what that season taught you or how it changed you for good.
That act of thanksgiving will turn the ashes to beauty before your very eyes.

Day 30
All Things Work Together

"He gives beauty for ashes,
the oil of joy for mourning,
the garment of praise for the spirit of heaviness;
that they might be called trees of righteousness,
the planting of the Lord,
that He may be glorified."
— *Isaiah 61:3*

"And we know that all things work together for good
to those who love God,
to those who are the called according to His purpose."
— *Romans 8:28*

"What you meant for evil, God meant for good."
— *Genesis 50:20*

Teaching

Ashes are what remain after something has burned — they represent loss, endings, and the things you thought would never rise again.
But God sees ashes differently.
Where you see destruction, He sees potential for beauty.
Where you see an ending, He sees a *beginning in disguise.*

"He gives beauty for ashes."

That word *"for"* means *"in exchange for."*
It's a divine trade.
You bring Him the remnants — the mistakes, the heartbreaks, the

losses — and He gives you something only heaven can make: beauty born from redemption.

This is not about pretending the fire never happened.
It's about realizing the fire didn't destroy you — it refined you.
You're not the same person who went into it.
Your compassion is deeper, your vision is clearer, your love is purer.
That's beauty.

Joseph understood this after years of betrayal, false accusation, and imprisonment.
When he finally stood before the very brothers who had sold him, he said,

"You meant it for evil, but God meant it for good."

That's the moment ashes turned to beauty — not when Joseph reached the palace, but when he saw *purpose in the pain.*
When you can look at what tried to destroy you and see God's fingerprints in it, you've entered redemption's territory.

"All things work together for good…"

Notice it doesn't say *all things are good,* but *all things work together* for it.
Even the ashes.
Especially the ashes.

Sometimes the hardest part of healing is allowing God to reinterpret your story.
You've spent years labeling chapters as "failure" or "waste," but heaven reads them as "training" and "trust."
The moments that broke you were also the moments that built something unshakeable in you — faith that no storm can take.

Beauty isn't perfection; it's perspective.
It's when your scars start shining because they tell a story of grace.

Selah — Pause and Ask:
"Lord, show me the beauty You see in the ashes I still carry.
Give me heaven's eyes for my own story."

Reflection Questions

1. What part of my story have I struggled to see any good in?
2. How has God already begun redeeming that pain?
3. What does it mean for me to wear a "garment of praise" instead of heaviness?

(Use the space below to journal your thoughts.)

_____

_____

_____

_____

_____

_____

Prayer for Seeing Beauty

Father, thank You for seeing beauty where I saw only brokenness.
Help me to trust that no season of my life was wasted.
I give You my ashes — every regret, every disappointment, every loss.
Teach me to see my story through Your eyes.
Wrap me in Your garment of praise until I recognize myself again — not as the one who burned, but as the one You rebuilt.
Amen.

Deliverance Declaration

In the name of Jesus Christ, I break agreement with shame, regret, and self-blame.
I renounce the lie that my past disqualifies me.
I receive the beauty of redemption in place of the ashes of my pain.
I am the planting of the Lord, strong and radiant.
My story glorifies Him — every chapter, every scar, every resurrection.

Action Step

Find a quiet moment today to revisit one memory that still carries pain.
Instead of asking "why," ask "what now, Lord?"
Then write one sentence of *gratitude* about what that season taught you or how it changed you for good.
That act of thanksgiving will turn the ashes to beauty before your very eyes.

Closing Prayer

Father,
Thank You for every person who has walked this healing journey with us.
I pray that every wound would be healed,
every harsh word would lose its power to define them,
and that their true warrior self would emerge — whole, fearless, and free.

Thank You for revealing to them who they are and whose they are.
Continue to heal them completely, Lord.
Remind them daily that they are partakers of Your divine nature.

Draw them closer to You until Your presence becomes their home,
and may they never settle for anything less than heaven's atmosphere again.

Teach them to trust You fully —
to rest in Your care, to find peace in Your promises,
and to love and protect the people You've placed in their lives.

May this be the beginning of a new chapter —
one marked by joy, strength, and unshakable love.

In Jesus' name,
Amen.

A Call to Action: Partnering in the Harvest

If this devotional has touched your heart and helped you heal, would you prayerfully consider helping us continue this work?

Every book you purchase and every item you buy from our faith-based apparel line helps us share the gospel, disciple others, and remind the world that **Jesus is King.**

Your support allows us to create more devotionals, translation projects, outreach materials, and ministry resources that bring healing and truth to those who are searching.

You can partner with us by:
👕 **Purchasing our books and devotionals** — written to help others find the same freedom and love you've experienced here.
👕 **Visiting** JesusIsKingWear.com — every piece of Christian apparel you wear becomes a testimony and a conversation starter for Christ.

Together, we can keep the flame burning — spreading His love, truth, and freedom to hearts around the world.

Thank you for walking this journey with us and for helping us make Jesus known — not just in word, but in lifestyle, boldness, and love.

Wear your faith. Share His love. Live His truth.

www.ingramcontent.com/pod-product-compliance
Lightning Source LLC
Chambersburg PA
CBHW070157100426
42743CB00013B/2950